The Perennial Philosophy

Series

World Wisdom
The Library of Perennial Philosophy

The Library of Perennial Philosophy is dedicated to the exposition of the timeless Truth underlying the diverse religions. This Truth, often referred to as the *Sophia Perennis*—or Perennial Wisdom—finds its expression in the revealed Scriptures as well as the writings of the great sages and the artistic creations of the traditional worlds.

A Guide to Hindu Spirituality appears as one of our selections in the Perennial Philosophy series.

The Perennial Philosophy Series

In the beginning of the twentieth century, a school of thought arose which has focused on the enunciation and explanation of the Perennial Philosophy. Deeply rooted in the sense of the sacred, the writings of its leading exponents establish an indispensable foundation for understanding the timeless Truth and spiritual practices which live in the heart of all religions. Some of these titles are companion volumes to the Treasures of the World's Religions series, which allows a comparison of the writings of the great sages of the past with the perennialist authors of our time.

A
Guide to
Hindu Spirituality

Arvind Sharma

World Wisdom

A Guide to Hindu Spirituality
© 2006 World Wisdom, Inc.

Most recent printing indicated by last digit below:

10 9 8 7 6 5 4 3 2

Library of Congress Cataloging-in-Publication Data

Library of Congress Cataloging-in-Publication Data
Sharma, Arvind.
A guide to Hindu spirituality / Arvind Sharma.
p. cm. -- (The perennial philosophy series)
Includes index.
ISBN-13: 978-1-933316-17-8 (pbk. : alk. paper)
ISBN-10: 1-933316-17-9 (pbk. : alk. paper) 1. Philosophy, Hindu. 2. Spiritualism.
3. Advaita. I. Title. II. Series.
B132.S6S43 2006
181'.4--dc22

2006017764

Printed on acid-free paper in The United States of America

For information address World Wisdom, Inc.
P.O. Box 2682, Bloomington, Indiana 47402-2682

www.worldwisdom.com

Contents

PART I

Introducing Hindu Spirituality

Chapter 1

What Is Hindu Spirituality?

I

If we take our existential condition as our starting point, we are immediately confronted by a paradox. Our existential situation immediately discloses two facts which, on the face of it, stare unblinkingly at us in stark contradiction. On the one hand, we find ourselves facing a world of objects which are material in nature, like the desk I am writing on or the chair in which I am sitting. These objects possess length, breadth, height, and depth. That is to say, they possess size. They also possess weight or mass. Simultaneously, however, we find ourselves experiencing them with something which does not possess these properties of length, breadth, height, and solid depth; something which does not possess mass, something which, in one word, is not material. This is the immaterial consciousness with which, or some would even say within which, we perceive these objects.

Many systems of philosophy have their origin in the attempt to come to terms with this paradox.

II

Attempts to resolve this paradox to our philosophical satisfaction have usually employed three fundamental metaphysical strategies: to argue that only matter is ultimately real, to argue that both matter and spirit are ultimately real, and to argue that only spirit, or consciousness, is ultimately real.

The first approach is usually described by the word materialism, when the word is used in a philosophically descriptive rather than a morally evaluative manner. It should be carefully noted that materialism, at least the sophisticated version of it we are dealing with here, does not deny the existence of consciousness. How can it? It is, after all, the existence of this very consciousness which enables one to even speak about matter. What is denied is not the phenomenological existence of spirit or consciousness but its ultimate reality. According to this perspective, matter constitutes the ultimate reality about the universe, and consciousness is an epiphenomenon of matter. Just as two gases—hydrogen and oxygen—generate water, which possesses a quality they don't, namely liquidity or wetness; similarly unconscious material elements give rise to consciousness. This scientific illustration has been provided intentionally because scientific materialism is the regnant philosophy of our times. The Hindu texts provide a more homespun example, that of chewing the betel. The betel nut is gray in color; it is usually placed on a green leaf with a slight touch of white lime and then consumed as a post-prandial refreshment. Once in the mouth, however, it turns into red saliva—a color which does not belong either to the nut, the leaf, the lime, or saliva.

The second approach is usually described by the word dualism, because, according to it, both matter and consciousness (or spirit) are equally real, and neither may be reduced to the other. This approach is not very popular these days but had many takers at one time, at least in ancient India. Thus Jainism accepts the ultimate reality of both matter and spirit, and so does the Hindu school of philosophy known as *Sāṅkhya*, which was quite influential at one time. This approach does not deny that there is something mysterious about the fact that such diametrically opposed entities as material objects and immaterial consciousness constitute the fundamental data of our empirical condition. It is, however, opposed to the arbitrary resolution of their binary opposition to one of them, as merely a form of monolatry. According to this view thought must follow and not preempt life. If two contradictory features characterize our life-experience, then we must hang on to both the poles.

The third approach, which emphasizes the ultimate reality of consciousness, is called spiritualism for the obvious reason that it resolves the contradiction in favor of spirit or consciousness. Once again, this approach does not deny the existential reality of matter, whose existence is too obvious to be credibly denied at the experiential level; it, however, does deny the separate existence of matter at the ultimate level. Matter is here regarded as the by-product of spirit. Just as lifeless nails can grow out of fingers throbbing with life, pure immaterial consciousness might well account for the epiphenomenal emergence of matter.

Although Hindu thought as such allows room for all three approaches among its many mansions, it has come to accord the pride of place to spiritualism over the centuries. This is particularly true of the systems of thought within it which base themselves on the Hindu scriptures, called the *Vedas*. These systems, which more specifically formulate their conclusions on the bases of what is stated in the end-portions of these *Vedas*, are called schools of *Vedānta* (*Veda* + *anta* [= end]). According to these schools, ultimate reality, to denote which they use the word *Brahman*, is ultimately spiritual.

III

The cumulative insight of the Vedantic tradition leads it to describe *Brahman*, or the ultimate reality, as *saccidānanda*. This word is a compound of three words: *sat*, which means reality; *cit*, which means consciousness; and *ānanda*, which means bliss. Inherent in this description are profound claims about the nature of the ultimate reality, not apparent at first sight.

Imagine being involved in a philosophical discussion about the ultimate reality. One of the first questions which will arise in such a context would be: does it exist? It is all right for us to formulate it as an idea, even a religious idea, but does it exist? The first word in the compound *saccidānanda* provides an answer to the question. The word *sat* means real and it serves to answer the skeptical thrust of the question: is it real? by affirming that it is; that *Brahman* is for real (*sat*).

If then we accept, if only to investigate the claim more thoroughly in due course, that it is real, then the next question likely to arise is: is this reality material, or material-cum-spiritual, or spiritual in nature? This point dovetails with the three approaches: materialism, dualism, and spiritualism identified earlier. The second word in the compound *saccidānanda* answers this question: the word *cit* means consciousness, which is to say, that *Brahman*, as the ultimate reality, is spiritual in nature.

If now we accept, once again as a prelude to further investigation, the claim that the ultimate reality, *Brahman*, is real and is spiritual, yet another question might arise: Is there one such ultimate spiritual reality or are there many such ultimate spiritual realities? Is there even ultimately, only one spiritual reality or many spiritual realities?

The third word in the compound *saccidānanda*, namely, *ānanda*, provides the clue to the answer here. *Ānanda* means bliss and this is taken to indicate that there can be only one ultimate reality because if there were more than one the possibility or fact of conflict among them would falsify the application of the word *ānanda* to such a reality, as the possibility of conflict among them would compromise its description as bliss.

Thus the Hindu tradition of *Vedānta* not only resolves the existential paradox in favor of spiritualism—it goes further and claims that *Brahman*, the ultimate reality, is also the sole spiritual reality.

IV

The description of *Brahman* as *saccidānanda* represents a point of agreement among the various traditions constituting the *Vedānta*; the question, however, of whether this one reality is personal or impersonal in nature has been a point of dispute within *Vedānta* from the very beginning.

The manner in which this issue has come to be framed within the tradition of *Vedānta* is as follows: does the one ultimate reality possess distinguishing attributes (*saguṇa*) or is it without distinguishing attributes (*nirguṇa*)? (One should not fall here into the error of imagining that an ultimate reality without distinguishing characteristics will be characterless.) In other words, is the ultimate reality personal or impersonal? Or, in the language of philosophy, do we at the end of the day conclude the discussion in terms of monotheism or the existence of one God; or monism, that is to say, the existence of one reality or Absolute? Is it more like ice, with tangible shape and size or more like the gases of which it is made, real but invisible?

This question, and the different answers given to it, have given rise to two traditions of spirituality within Hinduism, the theistic and the absolutistic. As this book is about the latter, I shall focus on it in the rest of the discussion.

V

The absolutistic spirituality of *nirguṇa Brahman* stakes the claim that the ultimate reality is without any differentiating attributes (*nir.* without; *guṇa*: differentiation) and it is this fact about it which in fact differentiates it from everything else!

According to this view three kinds of differences can exist among the objects encountered in the world. One can distinguish among different classes of objects. Thus trees are different from cars. These constitute differences of class (or *vijātīya-bheda* in Sanskrit). Then again, one tree may be distinguished from another, that is to say, one may distinguish among members of the same class (or *sajātīya-bheda* in Sanskrit). Finally, one might internally distinguish between say the trunk and the leaves of a tree. These are called internal differences (or *svagata-bheda* in Sanskrit).

According to absolutistic spirituality *Brahman* is devoid of all the three kinds of distinctions. As the word for distinction in Sanskrit is *bheda*, it is therefore described as *a-bheda* (without distinctions). This of course raises the obvious question: if the ultimate reality is without any distinctions within or without, how come we see all these objects and persons around us? Absolutistic spirituality explains such perception as ultimately erroneous, just as one might see a mirage without a drop of water being present in the desert. It also points out, however, that the explanation makes sense only after the mirage has disappeared and not before; the mystery of how that which is free from distinctions can serve as the ground for this world of name and form teeming with distinctions is best clarified once non-dual *Brahman* is realized, just as the true nature of a dream only becomes apparent after waking up.

This doctrine of non-dual *Brahman* may appear philosophically remote but it has a very personal implication for the spiritual seeker. If in the end there is only one undifferentiated reality, then, in the ultimate analysis, nothing can be apart from it, not even the seeker. The absolutistic spirituality of the school of *Advaita Vedānta* (as this school of *Vedānta* is technically known; please see appendix) embraces this startling conclusion enthusiastically and claims that the core of the spiritual pursuit consists of little else than the experiential (as opposed to a merely mental or intellectual) realization of this insight.

The formal way in which this doctrine is expressed in the school of *Advaita Vedānta* is in the form of the identity of *Brahman* and *Ātman* (*Brahman* ≡ *Ātman*). One part of the identity, *Brahman*, has already been alluded to so one may turn the spotlight now on *Ātman*.

One way of proceeding in the matter would be as follows. The sages of ancient India, in their search for the ultimate nature of reality, spontaneously adopted a two-track approach. One approach looked outward—at the universe, and sought to discover its ultimate ground.

The second approach looked inward—at the individual from the inside—and sought to discover the ultimate ground of one's personhood. Could we be our body? No, because the body changes but our sense of self remains the same. Could we be our emotions? No, they too change but our sense of self remains the same. Could we be our thoughts? Once again they change, but not our sense of self. Thus one was led to the "unseen self," the "unthought thinker" as the ultimate ground of oneself, the true self, which bears witness to all change but is itself changeless. This the sages identified as the *Ātman*, the ultimate ground of our self.

Then they made the sensational discovery that the ultimate ground of the universe and the ultimate ground of the self are identical, that *Brahman* is *Ātman* and *Ātman* is *Brahman*. This would be one way of understanding the word *advaita*, which means non-dual (*a-dvaita*). That is to say, *Brahman* and *Ātman* are not two. They are undivided. The expression "not-two" is used instead of "one"—although it might seem clumsy to us—to emphasize that they are not two things which become one, but rather that they were never two to begin with—they are the self-same reality.

One can now see why the guiding principle of this form of spirituality is contained in the maxim: "that thou art." You are what you are seeking. When we have the car keys in our hands as we frantically search for them all around, then we have in our hand what we are looking for.

This does not mean that there is no search to be undertaken. For at the moment we don't think so or know so. But it does mean that the search must be oriented in a certain direction. Although we have car-keys in our hands we have to be told where to look for them in so far as we are looking for them elsewhere and don't realize that we have them in our hand.

How might our spiritual search be oriented in this way?

Chapter 2

An Introduction to Hindu Spirituality

I

Hindu spirituality takes its first cue from right where we are at this moment. At this moment I am writing on a piece of paper on my desk. So let us take this as the starting point.

A moment's reflection will disclose an interesting fact about this existential situation, namely, that while the table, the paper, and the pen are material objects, the thought process which enables me to think of and commit these ideas to paper is immaterial in nature. Thus my existential situation brings two apparently disparate elements—as disparate as something material and something immaterial—together. This fact constitutes a major point of entry into the realm of Hindu spirituality. In fact it is so central to our existence and our experience of life that it deserves to be pursued at two related if distinct levels—that of the objective world as it is, consisting of tables, and paper, and pen and the subjective person or simply the subject, who is doing the writing. In fact these two incarnate the two poles of the paradox, the two horns of the dilemma. The objective world consists of material objects and the subject constitutes a center of immaterial consciousness. The division is neat, for the objective world seems to consist entirely of material objects, and the subject of immaterial consciousness. The division is thus neat—but not quite. For instance, the external world also consists of other human beings, indeed other living beings. We could choose to count them as objects too and subsume them in our objective world (although this is likely to give us a bad conscience). Similarly one could point to the fact that the subject possesses a physical body, which in several ways shares the property of being an object (although treating a live body, specially our own, as merely an object may also give us a bad, even a worse conscience).

There is thus some untidiness involved in the depiction of the existential situation as a center of immaterial consciousness confronting an objective world of immaterial objects, for some degree of overlap seems to be involved. The center of consciousness possesses a "material" body and the "objective" universe includes other centers of consciousness. Despite such overlap, however, and specially if we are conscious of it, this double configuration seems to capture our existential situation, from which we set out on a spiritual journey, rather well.

II

A question might be addressed at this point which might already have arisen in the reader's mind. It is this. Our own existence clearly represents a blend of a material (or if one prefers, physical) body with an immaterial (or if one prefers, mental) consciousness. Is it possible that this holds true of the universe also?

The question may not be as farfetched as it appears at first sight. At first sight the question might appear unduly speculative, for while in the case of the individual person it is immediately obvious that the person possesses a body and a mind and thus simultaneously illustrates the presence of both the material and the immaterial in one location, in relation to the universe we only witness the outside world, the body as it were. There is no "mind" identifiable out there in the way it is identifiable in the subject, or as present with the body. This could however be a matter of scale. If, for instance, we only examined a part of our body, say a subcutaneous section of the arm, it may not at all be apparent on a casual glance that it is part of an organism which as a whole possesses the kind of mental consciousness that we do. On that small scale one could perhaps proceed to determine whether that section is alive or not, that is, whether the section belongs to a living or a dead hand. One could perhaps also make this judgment if the subcutaneous section were physically removed from the hand; presumably such a sample removed from the hand of a corpse will look very different. The point to bear in mind however is whether with a sample that small one could tell if it possesses "life" or not; but because of the size of the sample, and not knowing how it relates to a whole body, we would find it extremely difficult if not impossible to postulate that it belongs to a body which possesses mental "consciousness." The parallel is obvious—if the external world known to us is part of a universe, of which it forms as small a part as a subcutaneous section of our forearm forms a part of the body, we cannot even begin to speculate what kind of "mental" consciousness such a "body" of the universe might possesses.

III

Most of us are probably familiar with the description of the universe (including those parts of which yet remain to be telescopically disclosed) as the "body of God" in a poetic vein. There are schools of Hindu thought which carry the expression beyond poetry into the realm of philosophy, and perhaps the exercise in the previous section helps identify the basis of this temptation. One is bound to be skeptical, however, of an inference based on an analogy but once we realize that human beings, at least initially, try to grasp the unknown in terms of the known, we would probably be less judgmental about it.

The idea of the big-bang as developed by modern scientific cosmology may seem to call it in question, but only partially. For attempts to explain the emergence of the universe from an egg, or even from primordial sperm, may really support rather than go against what has been said. Oviparous creatures again possess both a material and an immaterial component, as do viviparous creatures, and the attempts to trace the universe to such origins may constitute mythical forms of philosophizing to explain the presence of both elements in the universe. This is where the overlap in the distinction between the subject and the objective world referred to in section I also becomes relevant.

But to revert to the main point. The idea then that the universe as a whole might be viewed as the material counterpart to a spiritual reality, just as mental consciousness (or more theologically, the soul) may be considered as the counterpart to the physical body, while speculative, is not as unreasonable as it might appear at first sight. Even otherwise, since both matter and immaterial consciousness are given to us in our experience of the world, in the form of objects within it and in the form of other conscious beings within it, Hindu philosophy has addressed the question of the relationship between the two in some detail. The various ways in which the question has been answered may now be examined, as Hindu philosophy constitutes a useful propaedeutic to Hindu spirituality.

If we reduce all material objects to the general category of matter and the acts of consciousness to the general category of consciousness and refer to it as spirit, then the issue boils down to one of the relationship of matter and spirit. Since both matter and spirit are empirically given, three fundamental positions can be postulated on this point. These were mentioned earlier and are summarized here: (1) That matter alone is the ultimate reality, consciousness or spirit being an epiphenomenon thereof, a position which could be characterized as materialism. (2) Both matter and spirit constitute ultimate reality in their own right, a position which could be characterized as that of fundamental dualism. (3) Spirit or consciousness alone is ultimately real and matter is its by-product, a position which may be described as characterized by idealism (when the word is used metaphysically rather than morally).

IV

It might be helpful to offer a brief sketch of the schools of Indian philosophy before we try to contextualize them in terms of these three possibilities. Numerous attempts are known to have been made to classify or categorize the various schools of Indian thought from the seventh to the seventeenth century A.D.[1] A particular scheme promot-

---

[1] Wilhelm Halbfass, *India and Europe: An Essay in Understanding* (Albany, N.Y.: State University of New York Press, 1988), pp. 349-368.

ed by Western scholars in the nineteenth century for presenting Indian thought to the West, however, has by now gained wide currency. Let us adopt this scheme here for the purpose of this exposition.

According to this scheme Indian philosophy may be usefully presented in terms of nine schools of philosophy which are usually enumerated in the following order: (1) *Lokāyata* (or *Cārvāka*), (2) *Bauddha*, (3) *Jaina*, (4) *Nyāya*, (5) *Vaiśeṣika*, (6) *Sāṅkhya*, (7) *Yoga*, (8) *Mīmāṁsā*, and (9) *Vedānta*.

It is conventional to present these in two sets: the first comprising the first three schools, which are labeled non-orthodox (*nāstika*) and the second consisting of the last six schools which are labeled as orthodox (*āstika*). The test of orthodoxy in this case is provided by the acceptance of Vedic authority as a means of valid knowledge, the *Vedas* being the foundational texts of Hinduism. The first three reject Vedic authority, while the last six accept them, hence the divide. It is important to bear in mind, however, that this scheme could convey an exaggerated sense of discontinuity. For the first four of the orthodox schools, while formally accepting Vedic authority, do not base themselves on the *Vedas* in the same way as the last two. It would perhaps be more true to say that broadly the Vedic component of each philosophical system seems to gain in salience as one moves from *Lokāyata* to *Vedānta*, keeping in mind that this is a broad if serviceable generalization.

Thus it will be useful from our perspective to treat of these nine schools in three sets: (1) *Lokāyata* and *Bauddha*, (2) *Jaina*, *Nyāya*, *Vaiśeṣika*, *Sāṅkhya*, *Yoga*, and *Mīmāṁsā*, and (3) *Vedānta*. Note that the order of listing has not been altered, but the "decimal point" of distinction has been changed. The reason for this is that *Lokāyata* represents the school of Hindu materialism which accepts matter alone as the ultimate reality and regards consciousness as a by-product of it. The *Bauddha* school represents the various philosophical schools of Buddhism, which exhibit tremendous variety. The interesting point from the point of view of our present discussion is the position of Buddhism on the question of the soul or spirit (*ātman*), whose existence is regularly denied in Buddhism thus aligning it with the school of materialism, although in several other ways it differs from it. In this sense, it could also be considered "materialistic."

The next set of schools accept the duality of matter and spirit. Both are accepted as ultimate realities, although whether these ultimate realities as spirit and matter are single or multiple remains a point of disagreement. The *Jainas*, as well as the schools of *Nyāya* and *Vaiśeṣika*, consider both matter and spirit as constituting a plurality. All matter however is brought under a single category in *Sāṅkhya* (and *Yoga*), but at the level of the spirit a multiplicity of souls is still admitted. *Mīmāṁsā* is close to the *Nyāya* and *Vaiśeṣika* schools on this point.

Vedānta belongs to a third and separate category by virtue of subscribing to the doctrine that spirit alone is ultimately real and matter a by-product of it, or dependent on it, although the exact position of each school differs on this point. All schools of *Vedānta*, however, assert the primacy of the spirit, either as an Absolute or God.

V

If now we pick up the thread relinquished at the end of section III and examine the position of the Indian schools of thought on the nature of the relationship between matter and spirit, some interesting conclusions are forthcoming.

It is clear, for instance, that all the three possibilities—that matter alone is ultimate, or materialism; that both are ultimate, or dualism; or that spirit alone is real, or idealism, have been canvassed within it. Beyond this, the order of the enumeration of the schools shows a movement from materialism, through dualism, to idealism. Further, the degree of acceptance of Vedic authority shows a faint correlation with this trend as well. If we frame this theoretical discussion within the historical fact that of all the schools of Indian thought it is *Vedānta* which holds intellectual sway in Hinduism, then a philosophically idealistic orientation on the part of Hindu spirituality becomes obvious.

It must be remembered, however, that while it might be help-ful to view Hindu spirituality from within the framework of Hindu philosophy, it is not limited by it. For while it might be an interesting issue metaphysically to try to determine whether matter constitutes the ultimate reality, or spirit, or both, Hindu spirituality, in fact any spirituality, must address the pragmatic fact that both matter and spirit are experienced as given (even if ultimately one may be a by-product of the other). In other words, the fact that the spiritual aspirant begins with an awareness of both body and mind remains the existential starting point, whatever their ultimate reality. At this point we must also recognize that while the fact that the universe consists of matter (which is apparent) as well as spirit (which is not so apparent) may be a matter of speculation, the fact that the individual subject in the universe possesses their micro counterparts—body and mind—is not subject to the same kind of doubt. We shall build further from this point of relative certainty in the next chapter.

VI

Before this transition is made, however, the full importance of the point made towards the end of the previous section needs to be rec-ognized. Its importance consists of two dimensions.

The first dimension is provided by the fact that the main school we are drawing upon for providing the philosophical undergirding of Hindu spirituality is *Advaita Vedānta*. It has already been noted that the school is idealistic in its orientation, and in fact does provide a cosmic counterpart to the universe in the form of God, just as the individual possesses the spirit in relation to the body. One lead-ing authority, for instance, observes that in the system of *Advaita Vedānta*, "the qualified *Brahman*, if personified, becomes the god or *Īśvara* of *Advaita*. Like it, God may also be represented as the cosmic parallel of the finite individual self. . . ."[2]

---

[2] M. Hiriyanna, *The Essentials of Indian Philosophy* (London: Allen & Unwin, 1949), p. 164.

However, as we would like to present Hindu spirituality as far as possible in existential rather than speculative terms, we will not be invoking the cosmic idealism of *Advaita* in our discussion. Nor will we be invoking its concept of the Absolute, or *Brahman*—for the same pragmatic reason. Similarly, although the identity of *Brahman* and *Ātman* is one of the fundamental teachings of the school, we shall bypass it also in the interest of the same intellectual economy. For from where we stand the entity called *Brahman* could be a mere abstraction.[3] No such objection however can be raised if we begin our exploration of Hindu spirituality with that of *Ātman* as our own self, for it is undeniable, in the sense that if I denied that I exist, then the very fact of such a denial would only serve to affirm my existence.

The second dimension lies within this point. When we set out to explore our "spirit" we do not already "know" it, otherwise no exploration would be involved. Then are we not introducing a speculative element in our spiritual search by seeking it?

The question is important, and so is the answer, for it calls for an analysis of human personality that will be acceptable to all as phenomenologically sound. It might proceed as follows.

It was mentioned earlier that two dimensions of our existence are plain for all to see, as represented by the body and mind. Let us call the state of consciousness pertaining to the former as physicality, and the state of consciousness pertaining to the latter as mentality. At the moment we are experiencing both the states. There are, however, situations in which our consciousness becomes so fixed at the physical level that the mental level recedes. In a state of extreme pain or physical stress we may be aware of physical pain alone. Similarly we may be so absorbed in our mentality—so absorbed in thought, so to say, as to lose awareness of the body. This happens when we are so absorbed in reading that we lose all awareness of our surroundings, including the consciousness that we are engaged in reading. In other words, there are times when we drop the "body" and there are times when we drop the "mind."

[3] Ibid., p. 162.

But do we ever drop both body and mind? Perhaps one could say that we do so in the state of sleep. However, dreams involve mental activity. In dreamless or deep sleep, though, we are without awareness of either body or mind. So do we drop body and mind in deep sleep?

The problem is that we also lose awareness itself in deep sleep along with the awareness of body and mind. In what we described as physicality, the body becomes the sole focus of consciousness; in mentality, the mind becomes the sole focus of consciousness. In the course of normal living our consciousness is divided between both; in deep sleep these two and consciousness—all three—are gone.

The question is: what if one lost "body" and "mind" but not consciousness? Might that constitute an experience of the spirit? We know we have it in deep sleep in some form because in deep sleep we are not aware of either our body or mind, but on awakening from sleep we are still aware that it was "I" who slept, even though "I" had no awareness of mind or body. While absorbed in deep sleep, very briefly the problem is that we "know" that we are in the state of deep sleep but we don't know what we are. This search for what we are, then, is spirituality. For in the case of physicality we know that we are and what we are, and in the case of mentality we know that we are and what we are—when we arise out of these states. But spirituality is a state we need to enter into to find out what we are in deep sleep, for we know that we are then from remembering the experience of deep sleep. We also know what we are not then—we are not body or mind; but what we are in that state we don't seem to know.

The nature of the problem may be further explained with the help of an example. Let us suppose that you fall asleep on the couch after a long day's work. While thus stretched out on the couch you begin to dream. And in that dream you find yourself in the company of a sage who chats amiably with you for a while, and then remarks: "By the way, this meeting we are having here is in your dream." This constitutes new information for you because in a dream one is typically not aware that one is dreaming. One takes the dream to be real while one is in it. If you take the sage seriously, and he, let us assume, has inspired confidence in you, you begin to think out the implications of what he has just said. In the dream you possess a (dream) body which, until the sage spoke, you thought was yourself. Now, if you believe the sage, you know that you are not what you thought you were in the dream. You now know what you are not—but you still don't know what you are (until you wake up).

Chapter 3

How Might I Benefit From Hindu Spirituality?

The context of Hindu spirituality may cause some doubts to arise: Does one have to be a Hindu to avail oneself of Hindu spirituality? Does one need a guru to practice Hindu spirituality? and so on. And then, why should I practice Hindu spirituality and not some other form of spirituality.

It should be made clear at the outset that one does not have to be a Hindu to avail oneself of Hindu spirituality. Perhaps it is worth pointing out here that Hinduism actually discourages conversion from one religion to another. It does so not because it has some special gifts it will not share with non-Hindus, but because for it every religion is an occasion for universal hope. So one answer to the question: Who is a Hindu? given within Hinduism is: A Hindu is like anyone else, only more so.

Then does one need a guru? This raises the question: Who is a guru? We normally tend to associate a guru with a person. This is taking too narrow a view according to some. Anything which sets one off on the spiritual path could qualify as a guru: an event, a conversation, even a book. For, as has been said, there are really no gurus, only disciples. Even within the tradition of *Advaita Vedānta* itself—the desire to know the ultimate reality has been given the pride of place in its spirituality.

So there are no preconditions for embarking on Hindu spirituality.

But has Hindu spirituality something to offer which other spiritualities, in comparison, such as the Christian, the Islamic, or the Buddhist do not?

At one level, to ask this question is to compromise Hindu spirituality because Hindu spirituality is about spirituality—that is there is nothing "Hindu" about it as such in terms of a prerequisite. There may be something Hindu about it in terms of its specific formulation—but just as the effectiveness of a medicine is independent of a doctor's prescription to obtain it, so its effectiveness is independent of its Hindu origin. Nevertheless a few comparative comments could be offered on using Hindu spirituality as a starting point.

Christian and Islamic spiritualities work with a theistic framework. This is not the case with the kind of Hindu spirituality presented here (though there is, to be sure, a theistic Hindu spirituality). Again, the final results of the spiritual practices within Christianity and Islam may pertain to a post-mortem state. That is to say: their full results may have to be obtained in an afterlife. This is not the case with the kind of Hindu spirituality being discussed here. Its results, in principle, are obtainable in this life.

In this respect, Hindu spirituality is similar to Buddhist spirituality. However, to the extent that Buddhism questions the concept of a self, Hindu spirituality provides an alternative route. It uses the very sense of selfhood we possess to lead us in a direction in following which the old "self" is not so much denied as lost. To the extent then that one would assert the "I" in Hindu spirituality rather than deny it as does the Buddhist, one may consider it the best route for oneself. The person who wrote the following lines, for instance, might wish to take its route.

> I am with other people
> I join
> I belong
> I forge links
> I accept necessities
> I like being with other people
> Sharing my place with others
> But how far can consensus be taken
> Who am I among others?
> I am

Could it be that American individualism might find its fulfillment in Hindu spirituality?

PART II

Hindu Spirituality

Chapter 4

The Paradox of Body and Mind

The paradox of matter and consciousness, which confronts us as we confront the objective world, also possesses its counterpart in terms of our subjective experience of ourselves as human beings, over against such an objective world. What appears as a paradox of matter and consciousness now finds a parallel in our experience of our body and our mind. Our body may be different in being alive in comparison to inanimate objects of the universe, but like them it is also material and tangible—animate though it be. Yet it is also accompanied by a mind, which by comparison with the body is immaterial and intangible.

Once again, the attempt to resolve this paradox has also followed the triple pattern of materialism, dualism, and spiritualism.

If matter is the foundation of all reality in relation to the objective world, then my body could be taken as the foundation of my individual consciousness at the subjective level. The extending frontiers of neuroscience have served to strengthen the force of this materialist assumption.

> Attempts have been made by some scientists to work out the philosophical implications of neuroscience for humanistic philosophy. Thus, the idea of man as the neural man functioning in terms of neural activity has been advanced. It has been proposed to understand the whole gamut of human activities, appetites, feelings and thoughts, even thought-objects, in terms of neural activity. Such a reconstruction literally takes the human person to pieces and seeks to rebuild the fragments like those in a jigsaw puzzle. Different centers of the brain are connected with different activities and experiences. Selective damage to the brain leading to defective functioning has been extensively studied. For example Broca's and Wenicke's studies of aphasias are well known. So is Wilder Penfield's work on epileptics. Similarly various types of agnosias and apraxia have been

researched. It is not surprising that from such results "reductionist and connectivistic" views about human consciousness tend to be drawn. However, other results in neuroscience itself raise doubts about such suppositions. For instance it seems that even after commisuroctomy, cognitive and linguistic abilities may be retained, as if the parts of the brain worked within a larger field.[4]

The correlation of the disruption of brain waves and epileptic seizures indicates how such a view is strengthened diagnostically. That the analysis of the behavior of neurons and chemical changes and their relation to mental states has facilitated the pharmacological treatment of mental diseases is a well known fact. Thus the point applies not only at the level of diagnosis but also at the level of treatment. Nor is the applicability of this approach dependent on scientific advances of the modern West alone. Even in ancient India "some specific drugs like *saṁkhapuṣpi* were known for their therapeutic effects on some patients of schizophrenia"; and "*muktabhasma* was also known to help in depression," while the "role of food and drink and of mental dispositions overt and latent was much researched in this context."[5] It is striking that this principle was extended in India into the realm of the paranormal, for "some Yogic traditions believed that suitable stimulation of bodily centers can produce paranormal experiences."[6]

The point received its most thoroughgoing extension at the hand of the Indian materialists, who argued that as mental consciousness is not perceived to exist without the body, it must be taken to be the property of the body itself. This claim invites the objection that the physical body is only made of material elements, as becomes obvious when a person dies, and so obviously consciousness is not an inherent or a lasting property of the body. The materialists argued that although the material elements may not individually possess consciousness,

---

[4] G.C. Pande, *Neurosciences and Philosophy—Some Problems in the Light of Indian and Buddhist Philosophy* (New Delhi: Indian Council of Philosophical Research, n.d.), pp. 5-6.
[5] Ibid., p. 4.
[6] Ibid., p. 16.

their combination could give rise to it, just as a combination of primary colors produces secondary colors. Moreover, the body might possess mental consciousness under certain conditions and not in others, just as apple juice may normally not be an intoxicant but becomes so on fermenting.

The dualists, both in the West and India, basically tend to argue that, although body and "consciousness" are equally important for life, they are so utterly different that the possibility of the origination of one from the other cannot be seriously entertained, leading to Cartesian dualism and Leibniz's monadism.

The reader puzzled by the quotation marks around "consciousness" must be told the reason for doing so, which has to do with a striking contrast between Western and Indian philosophy. The distinction between mind and soul, which tends to be hazy in Western philosophy, is sharply drawn in its Indian counterpart. This produces the striking consequence that dualism in Indian thought can be postulated in two ways: in terms of a dualism between body and mind (where soul and mind are not distinguished) and another dualism which places both body and mind in the category of material objects and distinguishes the *ātman* from it.

This is a significant feature of Hindu spirituality and needs to be explored in some detail by distinguishing between two Indic words: *manas* (mind) and *ātman* (self or "soul"). The Hindu school of thought called the *Vaiśeṣika* presents an interesting transitional position here. This school possesses a materialist orientation, which becomes obvious upon examining its concept of self or *ātman*. In many Hindu schools of thought the self is treated as something spiritual:

> But there is nothing in the intrinsic nature of the self, as conceived in the system, which is spiritual as that word is ordinarily understood. The point in which it differs from other entities, whether atomic or all-pervading, is that it may come to possess knowledge, feeling, and volition, while the rest can never do so. In other words, the self is the basis of psychic life, but that life is only adventitious to it. The necessary condition for the appearance of psychic features

in the self is its association with *manas*. For these reasons, it would perhaps be better to describe the two together as really constituting the self in the common acceptation of that term. But we should remember that the conception of *manas*, taken by itself, is equally non-spiritual. The true self is thus broken up here, we may say, into two "selfless elements."[7]

However, although materialist in orientation this school is not actually materialist because the school accepts the *ātman* as a distinct ontological category.

It is when we turn to the school of philosophy known as *Sāṅkhya* that the implication of the distinction drawn between mind and soul begins to emerge clearly. According to this system, "mind" or phenomenal consciousness is classified along with the body on the side of matter, and mental consciousness is considered a derivative of pure consciousness. In other words, mind like body is also matter, but appears conscious because it reflects the soul, just as that part of the body of water on which the sun is reflected begins to appear luminous while the rest of the same body of water remains dark by comparison. Note that by contrast "there is not the slightest suggestion of an ontological distinction between mind or mental substance and the activities of the mind, or the attributes of mental substance" in the case of Descartes' metaphysical dualism.[8]

The significance of this point for our discussion cannot be overestimated. In Western conceptualizations, a human being is a complex of body and soul according to a classical Christian understanding; or a complex of body and mind according to a modern secular scientific understanding; but according to a broadly shared Hindu perspective "just as the empirical self is a complex of body and mind, the mind itself is a complex of pure consciousness and changing mental states.

[7] M. Hiriyanna, *The Essentials of Indian Philosophy*, pp. 90-91.
[8] William M. Indich, *Consciousness in Advaita Vedānta* (Delhi: Motilal Banarsidass, 2000 [1980]), p. 13.

Consciousness, mind, and body, however, normally function as if they were one,"[9] just as in the Western conception body and mind function as if they were one.

For the sake of clarity one might speak of a tradition of dualism in Hindu spirituality involving matter and spirit, with both body and mind falling on the side of matter, and with the principle of consciousness conforming to the spirit.

Advaita Vedānta adds a further wrinkle to this picture by proposing that the principle of consciousness involved here is a universal principle of consciousness, which only appears individuated on account of its association with a specific body-mind complex. In *Sāṅkhya*, by contrast, we appear as separate individuals because we really possess distinct bodies and apparently distinct souls.

Two sets of questions arise at this point: (1) on what grounds can we posit the priority of spirit over body (and mind)?; and (2) how could the one single universal spirit appear dispersed in so many centers like you and me?

The first point refers back to the general pattern in which the discussion of Hindu spirituality has unfolded; the second is specific to *Advaita Vedānta*. The two may be taken up in that order.

Of the three possible reactions to the question of body and "consciousness," *Advaita Vedānta* rejects the material and the dualist approaches in favor of the spiritual. The *Advaita Vedānta* develops this argument in two steps. It maintains that ultimately there can be only one reality, because if there were two realities then one would be compelled to examine the nature of the relationship between the two. But,

> Two distinct realities cannot be conceived to be related without the help of a third entity to connect them. Now, as soon as we think of this third entity (which must be distinct from the two terms it attempts to relate) we have to think of a fourth relating entity, and

---

[9] G.C. Pande, *Neurosciences and Philosophy*, p. 2.

also a fifth, which would relate the third with each of the first two terms respectively. Similarly, these fourth and fifth entities would require other similar media for relating them to the terms they themselves want to relate, and so on. There would be an infinite regress (*anavasthā*).[10]

Dualism is thus ruled out and so the question which remains to be answered is: which is it going to be—matter or spirit? We know that so far as the materialist position is concerned "starting with the existence of matter, it explains mind as only a function of it. But in thus starting the theory has already taken for granted that there is no mind, although it is as much an implication of experience as matter. In fact, we have no conception at all of matter, except as it appears to an observing mind. Believing in the existence of one thus amounts to believing in the existence of the other."[11]

However we saw earlier that one cannot subscribe to the ultimate reality of both. So the question is: which of the two is one going to accept? The Hindu materialist and the modern scientific materialist position has been that self-consciousness "can derive from the rearrangement of elements that themselves lack these qualities."[12] Such a view "assumes that more derives from less."[13] It seems to make more sense to assume that normally less may derive from more.

A meditation on the use of the word "mind" will help clarify the point. We speak of body and mind. There is however an occurrence in daily life during which we lose awareness of the mind—in deep sleep. We are not conscious of our mind in deep sleep, but on waking up we regain mental consciousness. However, the scope of our consciousness obviously exceeds the range of our mind, for upon waking up we are conscious that we slept. In other words, lack of consciousness is also a

---

[10] Satischandra Chatterjee and Dhirendramohan Datta, *An Introduction to Indian Philosophy* (Calcutta: University of Calcutta, 1950), p. 383.

[11] M. Hiriyanna, *The Essentials of Indian Philosophy*, p. 59.

[12] Huston Smith, *Why Religion Matters* (San Francisco: Harper San Francisco, 2001), p. 263.

[13] Ibid., p. 260.

state of self-consciousness, although in this state we are not aware of the mind because upon awakening from it we are certain that it is I myself who fell into deep sleep and lost mental consciousness.

What is more, we even lose consciousness of the body both while we are dreaming and in deep sleep, just as we lose awareness of the mind in deep sleep. Thus both bodily and mental consciousness appear to be subjects of self-consciousness. Self-consciousness persists even when we are not conscious of the self as either body, or mind.

But all of us possess our own selves. Does it then not mean that there exists a plurality of such selves?

We saw earlier, however, how there can only be one reality, for by conceding more than one reality we end up in infinite regress. So the question whether there is a plurality of selves gets transformed into the question: if there can be only one reality, how is the apparent plurality of selves to be explained?

Advaita Vedānta uses simple analogies to illustrate how this could happen. When we look into the mirror an image of us appears in front of us. And if there was more than one reflecting medium, more images would appear. In fact the number of our images which appear will depend on the number of reflecting media. The fact is also worth considering that although they will all be our reflections, these reflections could still differ from us in significant ways, depending on the nature of the reflecting media. Thus if the surface on which our figure was being reflected was concave, we would appear more bent than we actually are, and if it were convex we would appear as possessing more bulk than we actually do. Similarly, if the surface were dirty we would appear less clean than we are; if it were bright we might appear more radiant than we actually are. This use of the metaphor of reflection thus helps to explain not only how the one might appear as many; it also helps explain how these many reflected forms might also appear to differ from each other, as well as from the person who is being reflected. The problem we were faced with was: how could one single consciousness appear as multiple centers of consciousness; and, moreover, how could these multiple forms of consciousness also

appear to differ from one another and from the single unitary consciousness—for this is what is entailed by the empirical presence of a
plurality of different subjects? The analogy of various reflections of the
same object on different surfaces helps to make the point plausible.

The analogy can be further developed in a way which might be
helpful in spiritual practice. If we take this example seriously and per-
sonalize it, then what it means is that you and I are two distinct reflections of the single unitary consciousness as it appears in the context of
our minds. But as we experience it in our minds, although reflected in
it, it is being continuously refracted in this mind even as it is reflected
in it, for our mental attention is typically quivering with inputs all the
time. The various objects of the world are perceived by it; the various
senses of sight, sound, touch, taste, and smell are active in it all the
time, while old memories float by as we form new resolutions and so
on. In other words, that consciousness is dispersed in a hundred ways.
Nor is it a state of mere static dispersion like objects lying around; it
is subject to dynamic dispersion.

An illustration will help to convey this state of affairs graphically.
It is as if the moon was reflected in a lake choppy with wind. The
single orb of the moon would then appear shattered into a thousand
pieces. In fact all that we would see are these numerous shining pieces,
with their number changing all the time so that we wouldn't even be
able to count the number of such pieces. The correspondence of this
imagery to the way our mind functions in the course of daily living is
really quite striking. Can we ever count the number of sensory impressions we are undergoing or the number of thoughts going through our
mind? Not that no such effort has been made. It has been calculated
that an average person in a normal day experiences close to 60,000
cerebral events.

Another point deserves attention. If we do not already know that
what we were witnessing are the broken parts of a single reflection
as fragmented on the surface of a choppy lake, we are not likely to
draw this conclusion merely by looking at the shining, floating spots
of light on the surface of the lake. This will only become obvious once
the wind subsides and the waters have become completely still. The

slightest movement in the reflecting medium of the water will destroy the unity of the reflected image of a single moon.

Now it becomes clear why almost all spiritual practices emphasize the need for stilling the mind. How difficult the task might turn out to be can be imagined by meditating further on the imagery of the reflection in the lake. Not only can the surface of the lake be disturbed by changes in the environment it is in, as for instance by wind blowing on it or drops of rain falling upon it; disturbances could also arise by what goes on upon the surface. The wake of a passing boat, for instance, could disturb the surface. Not only is the stillness of the surface of the lake vulnerable to what goes on around it, or on it, it is also susceptible to disturbances from within it. Changes in the relative temperatures within the lake might set currents in motion below the surface, which may disturb the stillness of the surface. Or a fish might just suddenly pop out of the lake. All these dimensions from which disturbances on the surface of the water might originate have parallels in our life. Our mind is affected by the environment we live in. Who has not been upset by some friction in the workplace? Similarly, our own direct perception of the world bombards us with sensory inputs, sending the mind in ripples. Then there is the vast reservoir of our past life, and our dormant nature, lying just below the surface from which memories and impulses could emerge to disturb or even distress us.

We thus even lack the notion of a single "mind," being all the time not just in two but many more minds. The one time we might even momentarily achieve complete mental stillness, the realization that we possess such a mind, would be comparable to the single undisturbed image of the reflected moon on the surface of the still lake which we had never seen before.

To some the achievement of this stillness might seem the end of spiritual practice, but for *Advaita Vedānta* it is only the beginning. It remains to be realized that this reflected single orb of the moon in the waters is not real, although single, as all such orbs are. It must point to the moon in the sky from which it derives its glow. One could say that even the moon derives its glow from the sun—such are the hermeneutical risks we take when we embark on an uncharted meta-phorical journey!

Our unified empirical self thus points to something beyond it. But note that the "unity" of this self is different from the "unity" of the one moon in the sky, which appears as so many reflected moons when the waters are still, and into so many refracted slivers of the moon that it is even difficult to imagine that all of them form part of one single reflected moon image, when the waters are choppy.

Chapter 5

The Contents of the Universe

We cast a general glance at the universe—the objective universe—and identified the three main approaches of materialism, dualism, and spiritualism adopted to explain it as a whole. Then we took a general look at the individual—the subject—a psycho-physical organism—and identified three similar approaches to explain him or her. We may now proceed to examine the contents of these two—the objective universe—and the subject—with a view to determining whether a closer look at the contents of their experiences confirms or calls into question the earlier conclusions, which pointed in the direction of the spirit.

The example of the reflection of the lunar orb provides a point of continuity with the previous chapter by constituting the starting point of this chapter. In the examination of that example great stress was laid on the point that what is one could appear as many—as in the case of the one moon appearing as many reflected images of the moon on the surfaces of various bodies of water, or on the choppy surface of even the same body of water. There was also the implication that the moon itself—the lunar orb hanging out in the sky—is in some sense more real compared to the various reflected images of this orb. The moon, for instance, is not dependent on the images for its existence but the images do depend for their existence on the moon. No moon, no reflections. Similarly, what happened to the reflections did not affect the moon; but what happened to the moon did affect the images. Thus, when the image of the moon got shattered by a billow it left the moon in the sky unaffected; but the waxing and waning of the moon would be duly reflected in the image (if not tinkered with).

On the basis of these comparisons one could venture some tentative conclusions about the nature of the relationship between the one and the many, for it could be argued that this single-multiple dialectic holds the key to the situation. Thus what happened to the one moon affected all of the many reflections; what happened to the many reflections left the one moon untouched.

The *Advaitic* mode of thinking thus tends to be somewhat suspicious of the many in that, for it, this manifoldness needs to be examined closely in terms of its reality. In a relationship between the one and the multiple, the one tends to promise a more secure ontology, according to *Advaita*. This is a philosophically delicate point and one needs to pick one's way through the argument carefully.

The relationship of the one and the many needs to be carefully distinguished from that between the particulars and the universal. Thus, it is often argued that what we actually experience in life are particular colors such as red, green, etc. and one is asked, almost rhetorically: do we ever experience "color" as an abstract reality in general? This is a fair question. Note that we are not able to speak of a red or green color as "color" without a general concept of color. They would exist as they are but they could not be designated as colors, without the prior existence of the concept of color.

But to maintain that a general concept exists is no proof that what is conceptualized also exists. In fact, colors also provide an interesting example of the fact that what appears as one may consist of multiple elements. It is well known that secondary colors, such as green, represent a combination of two primary colors, such as blue and yellow. So what appears as a single entity may, upon inspection, turn out not to be so. In this way, both the existence and the unitary character of "one" could be doubted, contra *Advaita*. We are not so much concerned with a theory of universals or with the concept of unity (although these words are sometimes used) as with the analysis of reality. The distinction may be explained with the help of the example of the reflected images of the lunar orb. Let us suppose that we are working with five such reflected lunar orbs—in a lake, in a mirror, on a piece of metal, on a window-pane, and on a polished stone surface. Now, if we sought a universal for these reflected lunar orbs, we would postulate a "single reflected universal orb" (not a single orb) of which these are individual instances. But *Advaita* is not in this business, at least not at the moment. It possesses its own theory of universals also. But note the sharp distinction between speaking of a "single reflected universal orb," of which these reflected orbs might be examples or individual instances, and a lunar orb reflected in many (here five) mediums. One is here dealing with reality in general and not generalized reality.

In such a context the focus rests on different objects in different forms, and their relationship to each other and that out of which they are made or have emerged. It is in such a context that we must trace out the *Advaitic* intuition that the one may be more real than the many and that the one may be spiritual (and not just abstract) in nature.

Let us consider papier mâché and the various objects such as a cart, a house, and a doll which might have been crafted out of it. These various objects are made out of an undifferentiated single mass of papier mâché. They could cease to exist and lose their distinctness, but the one lump out of which they were made, the papier mâché, would continue to exist. The one, in this sense, is more real than the many and has more potential than the many, for while the lump of papier mâché could assume any of their forms, they would first have to become a lump before they could be molded into anything else.

Next, consider clay and the various objects which could be made from baked clay. These objects could lose their form but would continue to exist as clay. Raw clay as such possesses more malleability than baked clay, so that the one is not only more real and possesses more potential, it is also more malleable in relation to the many.

When one looks at all the multiple objects which characterize our universe one is then led to ask: what might be the spiritual significance of these manifold objects? One begins to wonder, in keeping with the *Advaitic* intuition, whether they might not also point to the one. Could there be some one substance out of which this universe has emerged, or, if the universe was always there, which pervades it as clay might pervade clay objects?

The question then boils down to identifying what all these existent objects possess as a shared feature. It turns out to be existence. Thus clay exists; the various forms that clay assumes exist; the various forms it might take exist (in the imagination); the various forms it might not take also exist as non-existents, and so on. "And when we think of a time or place where nothing exists, we are thinking of the existence of at least that time or place. So existence, in some form, is as wide as thought, and we cannot conceive of the absence or denial of existence."[14] Here again one is not thinking of existence as an abstraction (the *sattā* in *Nyāya-Vaiśeṣika*) but as a fact (*astitva*). And such existence is to be distinguished from forms of existence, just as one might distinguish clay from forms of clay. Note again that clay is one but forms are many and less real in relation to clay than clay itself. An animal of clay ceases to be an animal of clay by being destroyed, but clay remains. If we use the term "formless" clay to describe clay which has not been molded, to distinguish it from clay with form, such as that of an animal, then the point perhaps becomes clearer.

If we now look again at the universe with its many objects a curious conclusion emerges—that all of its various objects undermine each others' reality just as a lion of clay and an elephant of clay are both inconsistent with the reality of clay. The relative reality of the lion and the relative reality of the elephant not only relativize each other, their simultaneous existence as forms of clay points to the greater reality of formless clay. They do not contradict each other, but by their duality (or multiplicity) point to their less-than-real status in comparison to the unity of clay. Or in other words, any form of conditioned existence points to unconditional existence as the one reality, to which all the multiple conditioned realities point.

While the plurality of the objects of the universe in this way undermines their ultimate reality, the existence of a plurality of subjects does not undermine their reality in the same way because all of them are aspects of the same spiritual reality. This point is made

[14] Satischandra Chatterjee and Dhirendramohan Datta, *An Introduction to Indian Philosophy*, p. 195.

through a popular metaphor which describes individual subjects as delimitations of one undifferentiated spiritual reality, using space as an example. One can visualize a number of jars in a room. Let us imagine five such jars and label them jar A, B, C, D, and E. The space contained within each jar could then be labeled as space A, B, C, D, and E. Now let the jars be smashed. What happens to space A, B, C, D, and E? These spaces disappear into space, from which they were never different to begin with. Space A, B, C, D, and E had been artificially delimited by imagining the space contained in jar A as limited to A, whereas space is really unlimited.

Chapter 6

The Structure of the Experience of the Universe

In the previous chapter we referred to the numerous objects found in the objective universe, and from an analysis of their multiplicity, arrived at the conclusion that these multiple objects were less real than the formless existence, which made this multiplicity possible. It might now be objected that such a conclusion was partial in character because although our experience of the universe consists of these objects, it consists of much more. It also includes experiences which are less lasting than those of normal objects—such as experiences found in illusions or dreams. Moreover, there is also the case of deep sleep, when we do not experience the universe or its objects at all. How is the prospect of a Hindu spirituality in the light of *Advaita Vedānta* affected by the incorporation of such elements in our scheme of things?

One may begin by drawing attention to a particular feature of *Advaitic* thought, in which it differs from our everyday way of describing our experience of the universe. Normally when we say that I mistook a rope for a snake, for instance, and call it an illusion, we mean that we saw a snake where there was no snake. That is to say, the difference between normal and erroneous perception consists in the contrast provided by two situations; one which consists of the actual presence of a snake in one case and its total absence in the other (although it was imagined to exist). *Advaita Vedānta* takes a slightly different view of the matter. Considering what has already been said about existence in *Advaita Vedānta*, it will probably not come as a surprise to the reader that because the serpent appeared to exist, *Advaita Vedānta* takes it as having existed for the duration it was seen to exist; so the difference between the snake in real life and the snake mistakenly seen in a rope does not consist of it being present in one case and absent in another, but rather in the fact that it existed only for a flash in the illusion but continues to exist for a far longer stretch of time in the case of normal perception.

Thus objects found in both illusions and normal experiences are objects, but their objective reality does not persist in illusions as it does in normal life. But what about objects experienced in hallucination and dreams? A hallucination may be considered a prolonged illusion. In fact it is a relatively longer perception of the dream object which converts an illusion into a hallucination. But one could, however, wish to distinguish between two kinds of illusions or hallucinations: one in which the illusion has a basis in some existing object and another in which this is not the case. One may, for instance, mistake oneself as being chased by a serpent in two contexts: one in which one saw a coiled rope lying in a corner and mistook it for a snake, and another in which one felt one was being chased by snakes merely out of one's imagination—without it having a basis in any object lying outside, perhaps only as a result of having had too much to drink. These two examples may be distinguished from a third one, in which one is asleep and dreams of a snake, as opposed to the previous two examples in which one is wide awake. One could argue that the illusion of a snake based on a coiled rope possesses relatively a greater measure of reality compared to the one experienced in a hallucination. One could similarly argue that the experience of the dream snake could be considered relatively even more real than the experience of the snake in hallucination, in the sense that the dream, in presenting a dream-perceiver who perceives a dream-snake in dream-perception, offers a more consistent frame of perception at the dream level than that offered by it in an illusion.

These distinctions are, however, not important for the perspective of *Advaita Vedānta* being presented here because it offers a structural analysis of the universe based on the nature of the experience of the objects found in the universe, just as the argument in the preceding section was based on the number of objects found in the universe. In terms of this analysis it divides our experience of the universe into three categories, based on a particular feature of our experience of these objects, namely the fact whether that "objective experience" is superseded by another and the time it takes for such supercession to occur. On the basis of this criterion the nature of our experience of the objects in the universe can be placed in three categories, if the normal waking state is used as the yardstick of duration: (1) Experiences, the contents of which do not last as long as in the normal waking state. In this category belong the examples of illusion, hallucination, and dream experiences referred to above. The technical expression used for this category is *prātibhāsika sattā*; (2) Experiences, the content of which lasts for as long as our waking state. To this category belongs our experience of tables, chairs, etc, which do not disappear in the waking state. The technical term for this category is *vyāvahārika sattā*; and (3) Experiences, of which the content is everlasting, and never changes or, what is called *pāramārthika sattā*. This case corresponds to the pure experience of the previous chapter.

The three levels may also be explained as follows:

There are thus two orders of being, of which we may take the real serpent and the false as examples. If to do this we add what forms the common ground of them both, viz. *Brahman*, we have the three orders of reality usually mentioned in advaitic works. Of them, *Brahman* is real in the only true sense of the term (*pāramārthika*). Objects like the rope are empirically so (*vyāvahārika*) because, although by no means permanent, they endure in some form (say, as fiber if not as rope) so long as we view them from the stand-point of common experience. The being of the serpent, seen where there is only a rope, is described as illusory (*prātibhāsika*); and its distinguishing mark is that it vanishes entirely, when the illusion is dispelled. The distinction between the latter two kinds of reality may be explained in a different way also. The illusory object is given only in individual experience. When one is mistaking a rope for a serpent, others may be seeing it as a rope. Hence such objects may be described as "private." The empirical object, on the other hand, is "public" inasmuch as its existence, speaking in the main, is vouched for by others also.[15]

This explanation helps explain two points which had so long been bracketed away in the discussion. One of them is the problem posed by the disappearance of objects of normal waking experience in deep sleep. By applying the test of private versus public knowledge outlined in the passage just cited, it now becomes possible to suggest that as these objects continue in the realm of public knowledge while the individual is asleep, they differ from objects which appear only as part of a subjective illusion. The second relates to the nature of objects which can be imagined in terms of concepts or thought but can never be the subject of experience. The standard examples of these, cited in *Advaita Vedānta*, are the "hare's horns" and the "barren woman's son." The utter lack of reality of the son of a barren woman, for instance, in terms of experience (though not thought, even if it be self-contradictory thought or oxymoron), and the fact that the classificatory structure is based on experience, explains its exclusion from our purview.

The distinction implied here between existence and experience is worth noting. It is however the ability to experience which constitutes the criterion of reality, and existence and experience could either be considered as coterminous, or existence as exceeding experience in some way if defined differently.

One way in which the spiritual potential of this discussion of the structures of experience of the universe in terms of the objects experienced in the universe can be demonstrated, is to revert to the *Advaitic* intuition that the reality of the one is of a higher order than the many, for there is nothing to contradict the reality of the only one, while the many may pose a limitation for, or compromise, the reality of each multiple other. In this way, *prātibhāsika sattā* contradicts (at least temporarily) *vyāvahārika sattā* and compromises it, while

---

[15] M. Hiriyanna, *The Essentials of Indian Philosophy*, p. 167.

vyāvahārika sattā does the same to *prātibhāsika sattā*, only more effectively. The one *pāramārthika sattā* "reveals itself through all experience, and is neither contradicted nor contradictable."[16]

---

[16] Satischandra Chatterjee and Dhirendramohan Datta, *An Introduction to Indian Philosophy*, p. 392.

Chapter 7

The Constituents of the Subject

It is now time to turn to an examination of the subject with the same or similar lens with which the objective universe was analyzed. Just as the objective universe was examined for its contents, the subject can be examined for its constituents. Such an exercise will be carried out in this chapter. In the next chapter the structure of the subject's experience of the universe will be examined in the same spirit in which the structure of the experience of the objective universe was examined.

Any system of religion, philosophy, or ideology worth the name soon develops its own concept of the person. Early Judaism, for example, took tentative steps in this direction by developing the idea of a soul, although it did not distinguish between body and soul as two separate entities, and the body was considered the soul in outward form.[17] Christianity, however, developed a distinction between the two, perhaps under the influence of Greek thought. What this meant was that if one asked a medieval Christian thinker what the person of a human being consisted of, the likely answer was that the human being was composed of two elements—a perishable body and an immortal soul. A medieval Islamic thinker would also probably offer the same explanation, perhaps adding that the soul was not immortal but continually recreated by God (as the independent existence of a soul was taken by some as compromising God's omnipotence).

With the rise of the secular West, Cartesian mind-matter dualism dominated thinking for a long time until the rise of scientific materialism, which began to look upon mind as an epiphenomenon of matter—but highly significant in its own right. The work of Sigmund Freud (1856-1939) led to the identification of two compartments of

---

[17] John Hick, *Philosophy of Religion* (4th edition) (Englewood Cliffs, New Jersey: Prentice Hall, 1990), p. 122.

the mind—the conscious and the unconscious, while the work of Carl Jung (1875-1961) led to the identification of two layers of the unconscious—the personal and the collective.

In other words, the sustained investigation of the human person has led to the identification of different components of this person, although not without controversy, in the history of Western religion and thought. *Advaita Vedānta* also investigated this point, usually in the form of a search for the *ātman* or the underlying essence of the human personality. In a famous passage in the *Taittirīya Upaniṣad* (3.2.6), the various components of the human personality are successively identified as sheaths (*kośa*) such as those of the body, or food which sustains it (*annamaya*), vital forces (*prāṇamaya*), mind (*manomaya*), consciousness (*vijñānamaya*), and bliss (*ānandamaya*).

From the point of view of Hindu spirituality, however, a more critical rather than descriptive study of the constituents of the person is called for. One may commence with the pedestrian observation that just as the existence of the universe is self-evident to begin with, so is the existence of a self, or person, or subject. However, while the universe appears before us as a diversity of numerous objects, the person viewing it is initially given as a unity, possessing a clear sense of an "I." Thus whereas we could embark on the discussion of the contents of the universe straightaway with a recognition of its diversity, the examination of the constituents of the subject must start with an analysis of this apparent unity expressed by the word "I."

An analysis of the various ways in which this "I" is utilized helps to provide an idea of the elements it synthesizes. One speaks of "my house" or "my car," so that the person appears in one dimension as one who possesses various objects. These could be objects distinct from him or her, like a house or car, or aspects of his or her own self such as "my thoughts" or "my intellect." They could also refer not just to mental attributes but also to the body, as in "my arm," "my leg," and so on.

In other words, the "I" stands forth as an entity built up of possessions which are of three kinds: material, mental, and physical. These components, however, possess contradictory characteristics. Thus the material possessions could be viewed as belonging to one category and the mental and the physical possessions to another. Since the last two relate to the body-mind complex which constitutes the immediate identity of the "I," the material objects constitute only a proximate identity. They need not always be material, for one speaks of "my wife" and "my children," but they are separate from oneself in a way one's body-mind is not. It is possible to postulate an interval in relation to them which is not at least immediately possible in relation to one's body and mind, which constitute one's empirical identity.

Just as one's possessions can be distinguished from oneself and be made to assume a position in opposition to oneself, the physical and mental components of one's personality can not only be split away from material or other possessions, but also from each other, for body and mind, though together in one's experience of oneself, exhibit contrary qualities. It could be argued that "words that describe mental characteristics and operations—such as 'intelligent,' 'thoughtful,' 'carefree,' 'happy,' 'calculating,' and the like—apply in practice to types of human behavior and behavioral dispositions."[18] However, it is also true that the mind can remember things or plan or think in a way the body cannot. It is also possible to lose awareness of body-consciousness while mentally preoccupied, or lose an awareness of the mind in certain physical states such as deep sleep.

There is similarly a line of fracture even within the mind, as when I think of myself. In the course of such a mental process one part of the "mind" has become the subject that knows, and the rest has become the object that is known. Thus when one's material and other possessions were contrasted with oneself, one's self, consisting of body-and-mind was the subject and the possessions became the object. At the next stage, when one's self was considered as consisting of body-and-mind, the body could be objectified and the mind could be the subject. At a yet further stage, when one's self was identified with the mind, yet another split could develop within this mind, with

---

[18] John Hick, *Philosophy of Religion*, p. 122.

the result that it could be objectified in relation to a pure subject within.

One element, however, remained constant, through all this analytical choreography, the consciousness of the self within which these operations of the self's consciousness of possessions, mind-and-body, and then within the mind could be carried out. A good test of this is provided by the fact that if one tries to distinguish oneself from such consciousness, one still finds oneself left with that distinguishing consciousness.

If now we view possessions, body and mind, and contents of mind reflecting forms which one's consciousness assumes and so regard them as forms of consciousness, these can then be distinguished from pure self-consciousness. These other forms of consciousness then turn out to be less real in relation to this consciousness, just as forms of clay such as lions and elephants had turned out to be less real than formless clay or just clay itself.

Chapter 8

The Structure of the Subject's Experience
of the Universe

Advaita Vedānta's elaboration of the structure of the subject's experience of the universe has received more attention within itself, and at the hands of others, than other aspects, though for different reasons. It has received more attention for the simple fact that without the subject's experience of the universe there would be no universe to talk about, even if there was an objective universe existing by itself out there. So we have here at least a partial answer to the famous question: "Did the tree fall if no one heard it fall?" It may have fallen but one might as well say that it didn't because it made no experience-able difference. If the objective universe did not become the object of a subject's experience it would have no significance for Hindu spirituality, to the extent that the experiencing subject constitutes the focus of its interest, as at this moment.

The reason why the structuring of the subject's experience of the objective universe, according to *Advaita Vedānta*, has attracted the attention of those outside its circle is different, and may be explained by way of a contrast. That a human being almost daily experiences three states of being: those of (1) waking; (2) dreaming; and (3) deep sleep (= dreamless sleep) is a patent fact, on which all will agree. A point on which disagreement might arise, however, consists of their relative assessment. Western thought accords primacy to the waking state, and considers dreaming and deep sleep as mere appendages to it. The fact that it accords overriding significance to the waking state has been used by some Indian thinkers to contrast Indian philosophy with Western philosophy. A well known Indian thinker, T.M.P. Mahadevan, remarks, for instance:

Indian philosophy differs from western in that western philosophers philosophize from a single state of consciousness, the waking state, whereas India philosophizes from all of them.[19]

At this point one might feel inclined to raise a fundamental question: is not deep sleep a state of unconsciousness rather than consciousness? And if this is so, could it be credibly included in any enumeration of states of consciousness? The question is important.

Indeed the phenomenon of deep sleep is of special significance in this context, and this is perhaps best explained by bringing the experience of Huston Smith to bear on it. He notes "the different ways the two civilizations (Indian and Western) characterize dreamless sleep. The West does not assume that it includes awareness, whereas India holds that we are then more intensely aware than we are when we are awake or dreaming."[20]

Huston Smith then slips into the autobiographical mode as follows:

I battled my Vedanta teacher for seven years over that issue, I claiming that I was not aware while sleeping dreamlessly and he insisting that I was aware. When I pointed out that I certainly wasn't aware that I was aware, he dismissed my riposte as sophomoric. Think of how rapidly even your dreams evaporate, he said—most of them don't survive until morning. That much I had to grant him, and he went on to press his advantage. Dreamless sleep transpires in a far deeper stratum of the mind than dreams occupy, he said, so it stands to reason that years of (yogic) attention are required to bring its content back to wakeful memory. And what the yogis report is that dreamless sleep is a state of bliss, bliss so intense in fact that it is exceeded only by "the fourth" state of consciousness wherein *ātman* (the self's foundation) merges with *Brahman*. Were it not for

---

[19] Cited in Huston Smith, *Cleansing the Doors of Perception: The Religious Significance of Entheogenic Plants and Chemicals* (New York: Jeremy P. Tarcher/Putnam, 2000), p. 70.
[20] Ibid., p. 70.

the fact that we recharge our batteries every twenty-four hours by experiencing this bliss of dreamless sleep, my teacher concluded, the trials and disappointments of daily life would wear us down and we would give up on life.[21]

He then goes on to say:

My swami and I ran out his clock in this deadlock, but several years after he died something happened that brought me around to his position. To have my wisdom teeth extracted I was administered total anaesthesia, and in the improbable circumstances of a cramped recovery room with a nurse shaking me to return me to wakefulness, I heard myself exclaiming, "It's so beautiful!" Even as I pronounced those words, my grip on the experience had slipped to the point that I could no longer remember what it was that was beautiful, but that it was beautiful, staggeringly so, I can remember so vividly that to this day it continues to send chills up my spine. When I reported the incident to one of our daughters, she said that the same thing had happened to her, only her first words were "I love you," professed to a total stranger. "I'm so happy" was the variation a third party reported, while a fourth acquaintance reports that "this is so neat!" was the best his high school vocabulary could manage in describing the experience when it occurred to him.

The question this raises is, what prompted those ecstatic (I use the word advisedly) utterances in their respective modes of beauty, love, and bliss—three faces of God or the good? (I omit "neat" because of its adolescent vagueness.) Clearly, nothing that was going on in the empirical world. My own conclusion is that all three were reports from the state of "dreamless sleep" that the anaesthetics had transported their patients to and whose importance my swami had been trying to persuade me of.[22]

With this in the background one is now ready to share the structure of the subject's experience of the world with the reader. In its essentials the structure correlates the three states of consciousness

[21] Ibid., p. 70.
[22] Ibid., pp. 70-71.

in which the universe is experienced with three "bodies" that the subject is said to possess. Here again the paradigm of *Advaita* differs from that of the West in such a way as to require a word of justification. If one were to ask a Westerner how many bodies we possess he or she is likely to answer, once the initial puzzlement subsides, "Why, only one. The physical body." The answer from *Advaita Vedānta* is numerically different: three. According to *Advaita Vedānta* a human being—apart from the *ātman*—possesses not one but three bodies. "*Ātman*—the pure, effulgent, undiluted consciousness which is our essence—is encased in what the Indians call the 'causal body' which we experience in deep sleep. This in turn nestles in the 'subtle body,' which fabricates dreams, and that in turn is housed in the 'gross body,' which generates wakeful experience."[23] In this way "India's model of the mind incorporates these three states of consciousness in a way that positions them (figuratively speaking) in Chinese boxes."[24]

Thus the overall structure of the subject's experience may be presented as follows:

Subject	State of Consciousness
Gross Body	Waking State
Subtle Body	Dreaming State
Causal Body	State of Deep Sleep
Ātman	The Fourth State

The three bodies have already been explained briefly so one may now focus on the three states of consciousness in some detail, especially in view of the role it plays in the form of Hindu spirituality under discussion.

Although *Advaita Vedānta* also discusses such states of consciousness as fainting and so on, it is the ordinary states of consciousness—those of waking, dreaming, and deep sleep which are central to its

---

[23] Ibid., p. 71.
[24] Ibid.

analysis. It is on the basis of these ordinary states of consciousness that *Advaita Vedānta* draws some extraordinary conclusions, which then have profound implications for spiritual practice.

The discussion of the waking state might seem like stating the obvious but our familiarity with it should not prevent us from analyzing it. The key feature of it, according to *Advaita Vedānta*, consists of the fact that it is characterized by extroversion. The five organs of cognition—the eye, ear, nose, tongue, and skin—provide us with information about the external universe through sight, sound, smell, taste, and touch. One also proceeds to perform various actions through the five organs of action—speech, hands, feet, and the organs of reproduction and evacuation. Such action presupposes the operation of what are called vital airs or *prāṇas*. These are also five in number and include the movements within the body involved in such physiological activities as respiration, digestion, and so on.

It is, however, the psychological rather than the physiological dimension of our waking state that captures the attention of *Advaitic* thinkers. The word that corresponds to what we would call the psyche, as a catch-all term for mental activity, is *antaḥkaraṇa* or the internal organ. It is also called *manas*, *buddhi*, *ahaṁkāra* and *citta*, in accordance with some of its primary roles. Thus, as associated with the various senses it is called the mind (*manas*); when its discriminating faculty comes into the forefront it is called the intellect (*buddhi*); when its sense of separateness from all other human beings gains a sharp profile and it functions as an ego it is known as *ahaṁkāra* (ego); but when the fact that it represents the principle of awareness is recognized it is called consciousness (*citta*).

The waking state is characterized by the activities of a psychophysical organism such as it receives stimuli from the external world and responds to them. In the dreaming state the mind, which was in contact with external objects in the waking state, loses such contact and instead experiences internal states constituted by dreams. It is worth noting, however, that the dream appears as something outside the mind to the dreamer so that the experience of a dream, while it is occurring, appears as real as the experiences we have in the waking state. This observation bears reflection for it contains within it a statement of fact and the intimation of a possibility. The fact pertains to the realization that a dream can only be described as internal to the mind when we are in the waking state. The statement of the properties of the waking state are made by us while we were in that state itself. This symmetry breaks down when we are describing the other two states. The reasons why we only describe these two other states when we are in the waking state are obvious, but its obviousness should not obscure the fact.

Indeed it is this fact that allows us to describe the dream experiences as "internal," although even in a dream we see a world and even possess a body—our dream-body, otherwise called the subtle-body. Now if what we thought was external experience while we were having it—namely the dream—turns out to be an internal experience from the point of view of the waking state, might it not be possible that another experience which we think is an external experience while we are having it—namely of this world now with our physical body in it—might also turn out to be an internal experience, from the vantage point of another level of consciousness, which is as different from the waking state as waking is from dreaming?

The condition of deep sleep is different from both the states of waking and dreaming in that in it one does not experience any objects whatever—whether external as in waking, or internal as in dreaming. One also does not experience oneself as a subject. Does it mean that the experience of deep sleep is subjectless as well as objectless?

This could be said to be the case, or such could be claimed to be the case, but *Advaita Vedānta* offers a different perspective. It is usual for us to say upon waking up that "I slept well"; and "I did not know anything when I was asleep." The fact that I am able to say "I" slept well, implies that I was present in some sense during deep sleep. This is confirmed by the fact that when we wake up we do not think of ourselves as a different person, or as different from the person who also experiences waking and dreaming states.

The peculiarity of deep sleep consists then of the fact that there is no object present during it. Since our common concept of knowledge implies the concept of an object, and since this is not present in sleep, we say, "I did not know anything while I was asleep." Note that the word knowledge here is being used in its broadest connotation and not in the sense of merely intellectual knowledge. Thus deep sleep has no emotional content and no-one experiences physical or mental pleasure or pain associated with the waking and dreaming states, because these are derived from objects experienced as external at the time.

The phenomenon of deep sleep thus possesses manifold significance for our understanding of the nature of consciousness itself because of the exceptional nature of the case. The following points deserve special attention in this respect.

(1) We normally think and even say that we were unconscious while asleep. This is true as far as it goes—that empirical consciousness is indeed absent during deep sleep. But can it be maintained that consciousness per se is also absent during the state of deep sleep?

Much of Hindu thought answers that question in the negative. It draws attention to the fact that when "upon wakening from after having been sound asleep we say 'I slept well,' such memory of what took place during sleep supposes direct experience of the state of sleep. So there must be in sleep some cognitive mental state or process which is concerned with the experience of the absence of knowledge"[25]—a fact inconsistent with the assumption of total absence of all or any form of consciousness in deep sleep. Knowledge of absence is inconsistent with absence of knowledge. Or consciousness of being unconscious is inconsistent with total unconsciousness.

Advaita Vedānta goes a step further and insists "not only that [deep] sleep is a conscious experience but that it has the phenomenological characteristic of bliss (*ānanda*) as well."[26] This argument is based on the fact that we

have reflective cognition or memory of blissful sleep experience upon waking. The Advaitin argues on the one hand that it would be

[25] Satischandra Chatterjee and Dhirendramohan Datta, *An Introduction to Indian Philosophy*, p. 302.
[26] William M. Indich, *Consciousness in Advaita Vedānta*, p. 96.

absurd for him to try to claim that he perceives the blissful experience of sleep while it takes place, since he has already claimed that
the senses of the other means of knowledge are inactive in this
state. On the other hand, however, he argues that the immediate
awareness of the blissful nature of sleep experience realized when
we awaken cannot derive from an inference based on contrasting
our memory of having been in a state of disquieted knowledge prior
to sleep with the peacefulness accompanying waking. He thus con-
cludes that the blissful absence of suffering was actually revealed or
presented in sleep, although it was not perceived as such until the
knowing mind was reactivated upon waking.[27]

(2) When we are asleep we are not conscious that we are asleep.
This demonstrates that it is possible to be in a state of consciousness
without being conscious of it. This also seems to hold true of the
dream state, with "lucid dreams" constituting an exception.

(3) When we are in deep sleep we are neither aware of ourselves
nor of the universe. Normally we associate such a state with death but
obviously such a state is possible even in life.

(4) Normally consciousness always possesses an object. Deep
sleep reveals that objectless consciousness is possible—but not subjectless consciousness, as one identifies oneself as the subject on waking up.

(5) The profound significance of deep sleep in the context of
spiritual practice may be demonstrated with the help of a metaphor,
which corresponds to the reality that as we lead our normal life we
do not experience any moment of awareness free from thoughts.
During the waking and dreaming states our mind is never free from
some thought or another, while in the state of deep sleep there are no
thoughts. So a state in which there are no thoughts is possible, but it
also happens to be a state in which one is not conscious.

It is one of the central claims of *Advaita Vedānta* that a state of
consciousness is possible which is conscious (although one may not be

---

[27] Ibid., pp. 96-97.

conscious of it) and yet free from thoughts. The claim creates a credibility problem for us as we never seem to experience such a state in real life—when we are conscious our mind is full of thoughts, and when we have no thoughts, as in deep sleep, we are no longer conscious. But the phenomenon of deep sleep can be used to render the claim possible by means of a parable.

Imagine a fish asking a tortoise where he has been and being told that he has been on land. The fish would find such a claim incredible as the fish cannot see land. It lives in water and would perish if taken on dry land to convince it of its existence. It can only know of the existence of land by ceasing to exist! What then can the tortoise do to maximize the plausibility of his claim that land exists? He can take the fish to the bottom of the lake and tell her: "You see this flora down at the bottom of the lake as something which is solid unlike the water although covered by water. Now imagine that without all this body of water on top of it—that is what land looks like."

Take deep sleep—a state in which there are no thoughts—and imagine that state as one also of awareness rather than lack of it—that is *samādhi*. This possibility brings us to a new threshold.

Three states of consciousness were examined so far—those of waking, dreaming, and deep sleep. *Advaita Vedānta* supplements the analysis of these three states of consciousness with that of another, which it simply calls the fourth or *turīya*.

The three states of consciousness hitherto discussed—waking, dreaming, and dream sleep—are ordinary states of consciousness which all human beings experience. The fourth state posited by *Advaita Vedānta* is unique to it and is often referred to by the more general name of *samādhi*. The experience of this state results when the *ātman*, or one's true being, is experienced. In this state one experiences the inherent bliss of one's own true nature, which had been obscured by the thick veil of ignorance that kept one's consciousness trapped at the three other levels.

The experience of deep sleep is said to provide a foretaste of this state. In deep sleep the distinction between the subject and the object virtually disappears. One needs to say "virtually" because deep sleep is characterized by darkness or ignorance in which all distinctions disappear, but only temporarily. What is experienced is the unity of all things being dark rather than all being light. The state of deep sleep is oblivious to the world but exhibits no awareness of the ultimate reality, *Brahman.* The difference between deep sleep and *samādhi* is like the difference between being blind and being blinded by a flash of light.

The nature of this state must be understood correctly. The fact that it is called the fourth creates room for a misunderstanding. It needs to be realized that:

> Beyond *suṣupti*, both quantitatively and qualitatively different from it, is the bliss of *Samādhi* which is called *turīya* state. Though literally *turīya* means the fourth, it is not to be understood as in any sense numerically different. For example, when speaking of a coin from the first quarter to the last, with the first quarter, we say one quarter of the rupee, with the second we say half of the rupee, with the third quarter we say three quarters of the rupee. But when we come to the last quarter of it, we do not speak in terms of "quarter"; but we say One or whole Rupee. Even so, the *turīya* is a comprehensive whole and it is not to be expressed in terms of fourth of the four fractions.[28]

Thus, it is the one state that transcends and underlines all others. The fact that it is the one supreme state in relation to the other three states once again allows us to pursue the intuition of *Advaita Vedānta* that the one tends to be more real than the many, and that the many tend to undermine one another's reality. The three states of consciousness—the waking, the dreaming, and deep sleep—represent forms of consciousness experienced by the three bodies—the gross, the subtle, and the causal—while *turīya* represents pure consciousness. Thus

---

[28] P. Sankaranarayanan, *What is Advaita?* (Bombay: Bharatīta Vidya Bhavan, 1970), p. 40.

waking consciousness contradicts dreaming consciousness, while deep sleep contradicts both and is contradicted by both. Thus:

> A peculiar feature of these four states of consciousness, *jāgrat*, *svapna*, *suṣupti*, and *turīya* deserves to be noted. The first three are exclusive of one another. When one is awake, one is neither dreaming nor asleep. When a person is going through a dream, he is not awake nor is he fast asleep. In the sleep condition, there is neither dream nor wakefulness. Not so *turīya*. Like the fourth quarter of a coin which gives fullness of individuality and value to the rest of it, and to the coin as a whole, the *turīya* state is the undercurrent of the rest. Awake by day, going to sleep by night, and experiencing a dream in the midst of his sleep the same person exclaims: I am awake now, I slept last night, and I had a dream. This sense of "I" is continuous with all these three states, even though, as was pointed out earlier, *jāgrat*, *svapna*, and *suṣupti* are exclusive of one another. By what is this personal identity established in the three states referring them all to the same individual? This "I" common to the three states bears witness to life's waking experiences, to the dream events, and by virtue of the *pratyabhijñā* referred to earlier, to the persistence of consciousness in dreamless sleep. This awareness which underlies them all is said to be "the witnessing consciousness" or as it is called *sākṣicaitanya*. This *sākṣicaitanya* is omnipresent in our consciousness, pervades the *turīya*, the *suṣupti*, the *svapna*, and *jāgrat* states. It makes for the sense of identity—self. The *sākṣī* is present in all the states as their common denominator. It is not one of the states like the other three states. It runs through them all.[29]

One may wish to understand this on the basis of an analogy. Let us visualize a hill with a somewhat rising incline, let us then imagine three step reservoirs which have been built on its slope. Above the third reservoir lies the top of the hill where we stand. As we look down the hill the three reservoirs come within sight. We can then say that the view consists of three reservoirs laid out in majestic gradation

[29] Ibid., pp. 41-43.

from the summit of the hill. A little reflection will reveal, however, that although this is how the scene looks to us and how we describe it, the fact of the matter is that all the reservoirs are on the hill and would not be able to exist without the hill. The hill supports them all as well as the summit. We may walk along the pathway at the side of each reservoir on the next one and ascend the hill but it is well to remember that we were all the time on the hill while this was happening.

In the form of Hindu spirituality under discussion, the elucidation of the three states of consciousness not only provides a description of things as they are but also a prescription of where one might go from here and how. Crucial for both these understandings is the realization that the enumeration of the three states of consciousness is hierarchical in nature. It is possible to miss this point as might happen on reading through a passage such as the following:

> When a man is awake, he thinks himself identified with the gross body, as well as with the internal and external organs. When he falls asleep and dreams, he is still conscious of objects that arise from memory-impressions, and, therefore, the feeling of his limitation as a subject or knower opposed to objects still persists there. When he has deep, dreamless sleep, he ceases to have any ideas of objects. In the absence of objects, he ceases to be a knower as well. The polarity of subject and object, the opposition between the knower and the known, vanishes altogether. He no longer feels that he is confined to and limited by the body. But yet consciousness does not cease in dreamless sleep; for otherwise how could we remember at all on awaking from sleep that we had such a state? How could we report "I had a peaceful sleep, had no dreams," if we were unconscious then?
>
> The study of dreamless sleep gives us a glimpse of what the self really is when dissociated from its feeling of identity with the body. The soul in its intrinsic state is not a finite, miserable being. It does not separate itself from the rest of existence and does not limit itself by a feeling of the "I" (*aham*) opposed to a "thou" or "this" or

"that." It is also free from all worries that arise from hankerings after objects. The self, really, then is unlimited consciousness and bliss.[30]

Upon reading through the passage again one realizes that at the level of the waking state, consciousness is at its most diffuse—dispersed as it is among external objects and the knowing subject. Thus it is differentiated among the various objects, as well as among the varied internal states. In this sense it is differentiated at both ends—external and internal—and of course also differentiated between the external and the internal.

In the state of dreaming, the external world drops out of the picture—so consciousness is no more differentiated as external and internal. It is now only internal to the subject but still internally differentiated between subject and object. Nevertheless, relative to the waking state, consciousness is more unified.

In the state of deep sleep, this state of integration goes a step further. Not only does the division into external and internal not apply to it, as it did not apply to the dreaming state, but there is no internal differentiation of consciousness to be encountered in the state of deep sleep.

Consciousness is more unified in the state of deep sleep, compared to dreaming, just as consciousness was more unified in dreaming compared to the waking state. It can also be claimed that not only does it become more unified, it also becomes more homogeneous. Thus in the waking state it was differentiated into external and internal, in the dreaming it became only internal, and in deep sleep even this internal differentiation was lost and it remained an undifferentiated homogeneous whole. Yet another way of describing the consolidation of consciousness is in terms of the object-subject relationship. In the state of waking the subject has two kinds of objects it is related to: objects of the external world and objects of the internal world in the form of thoughts, emotions, and so on. In the state of dreaming the

---

[30] Satischandra Chatterjee and Dhirendramohan Datta, *An Introduction to Indian Philosophy*, p. 406.

object-subject relationship narrows down to one between the subject and internal objects only. In the state of deep sleep there is the subject but there is no specific object (unless one would wish to characterize nothingness as an object), so that at last the empirical object-subject relation is eclipsed. Yet another way of describing the increasing concentration of consciousness would be in terms of the distinction between knower, known, and knowledge, which characterizes all empirical knowledge, and to view the increasing concentration of consciousness as the progressive elimination of each element of the tripod into which consciousness is dispersed in the state of empirical knowledge. The point is best made by rewriting the three elements as known, knower, and knowledge. Then waking state can be said to be characterized by the presence of all three; dreaming state by the elimination of the known (external objects of the empirical world), and deep sleep with the elimination of all three.

This hierarchy of the three states of consciousness can also be visualized as the achievement of an increasingly pure state of consciousness, as one moves from waking state through dreaming state to deep sleep state. Thus, in the waking state our consciousness is the most cluttered; in the dreaming state it remains internal and can be said to be more subtle and pure compared to the waking state; and in deep sleep it is the most pure as it is free from its obfuscation by any division between subject and object. It is seamless and pure.

The spiritual path of *Advaita* has often been described as having the attainment of pure consciousness, as represented by the *ātman*, as its goal. In this sense, then, the doctrine of the three states of consciousness could be read as a statement of the goal of *Advaita Vedānta*, in terms of achieving pure consciousness or unification of consciousness. The ascending hierarchy of the three states can thus be seen as symbolic of this goal. Small wonder then that the experience of deep sleep in *Advaita Vedānta* is often referred to as offering a foretaste of the experience of the *ātman*, or *samādhi*. There are several parallels between the two: both states are characterized by a homogeneous consciousness, and in both one is free from sorrows and afflictions either of the body or the mind. There are also differences—in deep sleep one is dead to the world, whereas in *samādhi* one is also dead to the world but also awake to *Brahman;* if sleep is undifferentiated darkness, *samādhi* is undifferentiated light. But the two states are close enough for deep sleep to serve as a proxy for *samādhi.* This conclusion may be expressed diagrammatically in a chart.

One may now make the further point that the hierarchy of the three states of consciousness not only represents the goal or at least the direction of the spiritual endeavor in *Advaita Vedānta*, it also helps to point the way to it. It represents the end as well as the means; the goal as well as the way. To demonstrate this point, however, one needs to carry out a small exercise. One must now begin by reversing the hierarchy of the three states as discussed above in the following way:

At this point one might invite the charge of arbitrariness as one reverses the well-established hierarchy. It should be borne in mind however that the hierarchy of the three states of consciousness identified earlier was not an arbitrary hierarchy. It was a hierarchy based on a principle—namely the degree of concentration of consciousness represented by each state of consciousness. It stands to reason then that a different criterion might lead to the formulation of a different pattern of hierarchy among the three states.

Let us now replace the criterion of the homogeneity of consciousness with the criterion of degree of conscious choice available in a state of consciousness and ask the question: in what order will we rank the three states of consciousness, if the ranking is indexed to the degree of volitional choice the subject is able to exercise in that state of consciousness? It is clear that in the state of deep sleep we are not in the position to carry out any volitional activity. Even if we include the phenomenon of post-hypnotic suggestion being implemented in deep sleep, one would have to concede that it still does not constitute volitional activity on the part of the subject.

The dream state also does not offer much scope for the exercise of conscious choice, as a dream typically unfolds on its own. However, it could be said to allow for more exercise of conscious choice in principle, if one takes the phenomenon of lucid dreaming into account—or a dream of which one is aware that one is having it. Lucid dreamers have been known to be able to consciously intervene in the dream and change its course.

It is the waking state, however, which offers the maximum opportunity for the exercise of volition, compared to dreaming and deep sleep. In the waking state one can initiate action in both the external world of action and the internal world of thoughts and feelings, in a way not possible in the other states. One needs to realize at this point that Hindu spirituality refers to the decision to seek liberation as a conscious choice—one can continue in the round of *saṃsāra* or repeated rebirths endlessly. Hence, the identification of the waking state as the point of departure for the spiritual path is much more than a mere acknowledgment of the fact that only in the waking state is any volitional action possible. There is no presupposition here that because it is only possible to initiate any action in the waking state, therefore such an action will be initiated in that state. The universal acknowledgment of the possibility of initiated action only in this state is the acknowledgment of a necessary condition.

It should also be recognized that the initiation of action towards spiritual liberation must be distinguished from the actual action undertaken in praxis towards it. It is possible, for instance, to resolve to seek liberation as a result of a dream—either because one was mystically initiated in it or because of some other experience in that state. But it is hardly possible to commence one's actual *sādhanā* as such in a dream. That, at least normally, must take place in the waking state. In this sense another aspect of the waking state is worth noting—the sense of awakening associated with it. Often the experience of spiritual realization is described in terms of the metaphor of awakening, the designation "Buddha" constituting a famous illustration of this. There is, however, the more striking point that not only the beginning of the *sādhanā* but the achievement of its end—*samādhi*—also has to occur in the waking state to be fully salvific. It has been famously remarked that those who have awakened in a dream have not awakened from it.

Chapter 9

The Logic of the Spiritual Path

If the basic premise of *Advaita Vedānta* consists of the claim that the experience of our ordinary daily life does not exhaust reality, and of the further claim that this missing dimension is capable of becoming accessible through spiritual practice, then what it needs to offer to us is a convenient shorthand statement of this claim rather than a long paragraph such as this one.

It offers such a shorthand description in the interpretation it offers of the sacred Hindu symbol:

AUM

This sacred sound goes back to at least the tenth century B.C. How it acquired a sacred character is not known with scholarly certainty but acquire it it did. It is an indication of the measure of its sanctity that it is considered a sacred sound in all the other religions of Indian origin: Buddhism, Jainism, and Sikhism (although the evidence of its acceptance in the *Theravāda* form of Buddhism may be a point of debate). It has remained a sacred sound to this date and is often chanted to mark the start and the conclusion of a religious occasion.

This aural symbol is thus virtually the property of the Indic religious tradition, with different religions imparting to it their own interpretation. The same is true of Hinduism, which given its pluralistic character is also subject to a wide variety of interpretations.

One aspect of this sound symbol has been particularly helpful in facilitating its various interpretations, apart from its sacred character in general. This consists of the fact that according to Sanskrit grammar the sound AUM consists of three distinct syllables—A, U, and M. This triadic character of the sound enables it to accommodate a variety of trinities. In Hindu theism, for instance, the sound is used to represent the three gods of the so-called Hindu trinity: *Brahmā*, the god of creation, *Viṣṇu*, the god of preservation, and *Śiva*, the god of termination. Indian Christians have been known to use the sound to represent the Christian trinity.

This tripartite aspect of the sound AUM is also used in *Advaita Vedānta* to represent the three states of consciousness dealt with in extenso in a previous chapter—those of waking, dreaming, and deep sleep—in the following manner:

Waking	A
Dreaming	U
Deep sleep	M

The reader will realize that this pattern of association has the merit of reducing the entire range of our experience of life into a single symbol. This could be considered the spiritual equivalent of the Einsteinian equation $e=mc^2$, equally sensational in its brevity.

All the experiences we have during the course of a day, and even the course of a life, are experienced by us in one of the three states of consciousness: waking, dreaming, or deep sleep. Interpreted in this way the symbol offers a summary statement of the whole of our normal everyday life. In order to serve a spiritual purpose, however, the symbol must do something more than tersely summarize all that we experience in life; it must also point to that which remains to be experienced in order to complete our experience of life. In other words, the symbol must also find room for symbolizing the fourth state of consciousness as well.

Advaita Vedānta achieves this result by pointing out that although the AUM sound seems to contain only three parts in terms of the three syllables, the silence which follows its utterance could also be interpreted as part of it for our purposes. Viewed in this way the AUM sound could be said to consist of two parts—the audible part represented by the three syllables, and the inaudible part represented by the silence which follows it. This inaudible part then may be taken to stand for the fourth state of consciousness as follows:

A	Waking State
U	Dreaming State
M	Deep Sleep State
Silence	Fourth State

These correspondences border on the felicitous because just like the silence that may be considered part of the AUM sound and is yet qualitatively apart from it, the fourth state may be counted as one of the states of consciousness but it is also unique in its own way.

In terms of this analysis the AUM sound then comes to represent both life as it is and life as we want it to be—to include the experience of the fourth and thus combine both diagnosis and prescription in one.

But it does more. It also doubles as the medicine itself in the following manner, if we continue to employ medical imagery. As will be explained in more detail in a later chapter, once we start on the path of spiritual practice the AUM sound, whether chanted audibly or inaudibly, serves as a useful instrument to concentrate the mind. That is to say, it can be used as a mantra to concentrate the mind so as to facilitate the attainment of *samādhi*. Thus, while as a symbol it serves to define the end of spiritual practice, as a mantra it also provides a means for such practice. Its ability to represent both the end as well as the means of spiritual life makes it spiritually even more potent.

This entire book up to this point can then be summarized in one sound symbol—AUM.

Chapter **10**

The Promise of the Spiritual Path

It might be worthwhile to cast another glance at the landscape laid out in the previous chapter, lest one not see the wood for the trees. This second look may be prefaced with the following question: what is the fundamental claim of *Advaita Vedānta* in respect to spirituality, shorn of its doctrinal frills? Or as the Americans ask: what is the bottom line?

In a way the spiritual claim staked by *Advaita Vedānta* is quite simple and can be stated quite simply. It is this: that our experience of ordinary life as it is daily lived does not exhaust our experience of reality.

Let us pause for a moment to examine the nature of this claim. We experience what life offers us in the course of the three states of consciousness and have perhaps formed the impression that what happens to us in these three states is all that life has to offer. It is the claim of Hindu spirituality that there is more to life; that by living life as we know it as confined to the three states of consciousness we are missing out on something. Nor is what is being missed something trivial; in fact it is potentially so significant that it may make us reevaluate all the other states of consciousness in its new light.

A couple of examples might help reinforce this claim. Let us suppose that one was born and brought up on the banks of a mighty river. One's view of the world as a child therefore came to be dominated by a duality of firm land on which one stood and had one's house, and a flowing body of water, which one beheld standing on this terra firma—sometimes even in awe. Such then was the environment one grew up in—with a vision of the world dominated by firm land and flowing water. Let us now suppose that as one grew up one's curiosity about one's environment increased and one began to ask questions of the elders—about one's surroundings, and further, that in the course of these queries one was told that although one beheld a mighty river flowing all the time, underneath it also lay solid land. One would be incredulous at first, but were one of the elders to take the trouble to go out on a boat so that one could dive on one's own and verify the claim for oneself, one's doubts would be dispelled. When one now stepped on the shore one would do so bathed in a new realization of reality. For as one put one's foot on the shore one would suddenly realize that the solid dry land on which one stood now extended without a break to the bottom of the river—that it was the same land on which you stood and the river flowed, despite the immense difference on the surface as one surveyed it—between solid land and flowing water. One's appreciation of one's environment would have been revolutionized by the realization that the river had a river bed and that the river bed was just like the land one stood on, except for the fact that it was submerged in water. Perhaps the *Advaitic* claim involves a similar eureka experience.

Or perhaps one had grown-up as a child inordinately fond of movies and one's world of experience consisted of all these images one watched on the screen—images in color, and images in black and white, and images of war and of gardens and palaces and heroes and beautiful women and lovely children . . . until one day one stayed on to watch not only the end of the picture but the whole show and saw the blank screen, all white, for the first time. Until then one had no idea that the viewing of all the images one saw involved the presence of a screen. And it would all have seemed so improbable as the screen was blank, and the films had images. The screen was white, the films were full of colors; the screen just sat or stood there unmoving, doing nothing, motionless—while the films were so full of action, all kinds of action. And it was only gradually that one was able to put the film and the screen together—it even took one some days, even to have some sense of one's discovery and not to doubt it. Maybe the experience which Hindu spirituality culminates in is something like that.

Even as grown-ups we might make discoveries about our environment which might revolutionize our understanding of it, even when we are individually familiar with every element of it—it is the way all that knowledge comes together that is transformative. It could happen as follows. We have just come out of a building and stepped onto the road when all of a sudden we find ourselves caught between two groups who are advancing menacingly towards each other, both of whom are vigorously waving us off the road. We panic. We see a street fight on the verge of breaking out and one of us is about to dart to the phone to call the police. Suddenly we feel a gentle tap on the shoulder and the person puts a finger to his lips and points us in the direction of a tree whose branches are swarming with people. For a moment we feel that we are in even greater trouble than we originally thought, when suddenly we see the filming camera and we realize that a film is being shot. And soon we are enjoying the shooting.

Or we are a student and late for class. As we hurriedly settle down in the seat we find a questionnaire in front of us and hurriedly start filling it in. Then we come to the last line and it says: this is a sample, you don't need to fill this in.

Chapter 11

The AUM Sound and the Logic of Spiritual Practice

Spiritual practice is comparable to a cleaning operation in some ways, especially as visualized in *Advaita Vedānta*. Let us suppose that a room is cluttered with dust and needs to be cleaned up. How then do we strategize such an operation?

Before embarking on a clean-up we often put on a protective garb. Then we proceed to gather all the dust in a heap either in the center or in the corner of a room. Finally, in one quick operation, we remove this assembled mass of dust and the room is cleaned up. Two points are worth reflecting on in terms of this operation. The first is that once the room is cleaned up, more space has been created. The effect is of course far more dramatic if the room was full of cartons and they were all removed, but the fact still holds true for our more humble operation. But the second point is even more striking—that in order to create more space all we had to do was to remove things which cluttered it. That is to say—the space was already there in the room. We did not create it nor did we bring it in from outside. Although the making of space sounds like a positive act, it was achieved by a negative modus operandi, by removing things from the room.

This example serves as a helpful illustration of spiritual practice because it enables one to clarify several aspects of the spiritual practice of *Advaita Vedānta* that might initially appear puzzling. The use of the word meditation to describe such spiritual practices is a case in point. Meditation seems to imply the concept of meditation on something. Thus we say that we are meditating on a course of action—that is, thinking about it. Another frequent use of the word also provides a useful clue. Sometimes it is said that so-and-so is meditating on resigning, or even committing suicide. This conveys the additional sense that it implies not merely thinking but thinking repeatedly about something. Another way the word is used is to ask someone who is sitting quietly in a corner: "Are you meditating?" If we bring all these uses of the word together then it seems to imply (1) sequestering or detaching oneself; and (2) thinking about something repeatedly in such a state.

This process of thinking of the same thing repeatedly, even continuously if possible, is called concentration. The immensity of the enterprise represented by this word should not be underestimated. Just to get an idea of what might be involved all one needs to do is to sit back and take stock of the thoughts passing through one's mind—the word thought being employed to cover all forms of mental activity. As soon as one begins to witness this flow of thoughts through the mind, the significance of the term "stream of consciousness" and all the stuff floating on it is brought home. The "stream of consciousness" novels, such as James Joyce's *Ulysses* convey a good idea of what is intended. These thoughts—these mental acts—are like a flood—a river in spate. It is not even possible to stop them right away. It would be like trying to build a dam while a river is in spate—it would be swept way. The way to control it is to divert it into a particular channel or a gorge—and that is what concentration is all about.

These uses provide parallels with the clean-up operation described earlier. The clean-up man dons his work clothes and thereby detaches himself from all other persons, who continue to work in their suits. Similarly, the meditator detaches himself or herself from others. Then the clean-up man repeatedly lifts dust from all parts of the room and concentrates it in one place. Similarly, the meditator draws his mind repeatedly from all things to concentrate on (in this case) the AUM sound. Then, we come to the final part of the clean-up operation— that of removing the collected dust from the room, the equivalent to which would be removing the thoughts concentrated in the AUM mantra from the mind.

This act—not covered by the usual sense of the word "meditation"—is in fact the most crucial part of "meditation" as understood in Advaita Vedānta. In order to understand why this is so, we have to revert to a consideration of the point made earlier—that spiritual practice is to be carried out in the waking state, although its goal is to reach a state of consciousness represented by the state of deep sleep.

How does this insight translate in actual practice? One basic feature of the state of deep sleep needs to be recognized at this point, namely, that in the state of deep sleep the consciousness, or more colloquially the mind, is without thoughts. The word thoughts is being used here in its broadest acceptation—as representing all forms of mental activity, so that mental impressions, sensory inputs, feeling, and so on, also count as thoughts. In practical terms, then, the idea that we wish to reach the state symbolized by deep sleep in the waking state means that our aim is to empty the mind of all thoughts. How this state can be brought about through a meditation on AUM is as follows. One sits in a quiet dark place so that sensory stimuli are reduced to a minimum. Then one starts concentrating on the AUM sound chanted mentally, with such concentration that the AUM sound either absorbs or drives away all other thoughts, so that the mind becomes identical with the AUM sound, and the AUM sound with the mind. This would then mean in principle that when the AUM sound as chanted in the mind subsides, all thoughts should cease as the AUM dies down. Then the ensuing silence will represent the realization of the fourth state.

That's the theory, although it remains true that the perfect meditator will need to chant the AUM sound only once—either audibly or in the mind—to attain *samādhi*. What we ordinary mortals achieve by this exercise is the attenuation rather than the cessation of the flow of thoughts. In order to ensure that the attenuation ultimately leads to a cessation of thoughts one needs to proceed as follows: if a measure of concentration on the AUM has been successfully achieved, a point will then arise when the flow of thoughts will largely consist of AUM sounds chanted mentally. The word "largely" has been used advisedly because if complete concentration has been achieved then the AUM thought (the AUM sound mentally chanted) will be the only thought passing through the mind. However, as most of us are likely to achieve relatively higher degrees of concentration on the AUM thought rather than absolute concentration on it, it might be more appropriate to describe the state of mind as one which largely consists of AUM thoughts passing through it.

Such AUM thoughts can be viewed as consisting of two elements—the AUM thought and the silence which follows the AUM thought, before the next AUM thought surfaces in the mind. The aim of the final goal of meditation can now be operationally defined as follows: lengthening and deepening of the silent gap between two recurring AUM thoughts. This is the crack in the universe that will open us up to the ultimate. This is the thin edge of the wedge with which the secrets of the universe may be prised open.

An illustration might once again help explain the point. Let us suppose we were watching a movie on the screen and are then told that the reality underlying the images is the screen which we have never seen, but should. However, all that we have in front of us is the movie. Whenever the movie ends the lights of the room are also immediately switched off so there is no hope of our seeing the screen as it is except through the movie—and until we see it we have just to take it on faith that there is a screen underlying the movie.

How then can we possibly see the screen while the movie is still on? We begin by slowing down the speed with which the reel is being projected until it slows down so much that as the film moves, in the course of projection, we are able to feel one still frame being followed by another. After all, the sense of movement on the screen is an illusion generated by the reel being projected at a certain speed. The reel is merely a series of stills.

The gap between the two AUM sounds is like the space between the two stills. As one still is replaced by another there is a brief moment when the screen appears as it is—a very brief moment no doubt but certainly there. As the film slows down we will begin to get momentary glimpses of the screen in this way and once the film has really slowed down so that the movement from one still to another is perceptible, even more of the screen will become visible. Were the film to stop running we would be able to see the screen for what it is. The great challenge of the spiritual path in these terms is to smash the projector called the mind.

One special point in terms of actual practice needs to be specially and separately noted. It was mentioned earlier that the final goal of meditation is to increase the gap of silence between two AUM sounds. One's initial impulse might be to focus one's mind on this gap so as to increase it. Such a procedure, however, would be self-defeating because if the mind is made to focus on the gap, it is no longer a gap between two thoughts but rather a gap-thought. So in order to increase the gap between two thoughts—in this case two AUM thoughts—the way to proceed is to focus the mind on the AUM thought itself so completely that the mind becomes the AUM thought and the AUM thought becomes the mind. Then, when the AUM thought subsides, mental activity will cease along with it—opening up the gap between two AUM thoughts.

The metaphor of the stream of consciousness was introduced in an earlier chapter. In the course of developing it, the passage of thoughts through the mind was compared to the onrush of flooding waters. This is how our mind functions in normal life, bombarded as it is from all sides with all kinds of inputs, like rainwater flowing into the river and swelling it to a flood.

The first step then is to control the flow of these waters before one can think of stopping them. Similarly, thoughts have to be controlled before they can be stopped. Thus, focusing the mind on one thought is like directing the flood waters into a gorge.

Let us now imagine that lower down along this gorge there is a dam that will finally contain the flow of the water, and the dry river bed will then stand revealed beyond this dam. Note that it is not possible to construct a dam in the face of the raging waters of the flood. They must first be allowed to flow, then be made to flow in a gorge, and then be stopped by a dam.

There are two points to this analogy. The first is that a stage preliminary to that of meditation consists of simply witnessing the flow of thoughts through the mind, without trying to interfere with their flood in any way, on the analogy of letting the flood waters rage until the river approaches the gorge. The other is that just as the raging waters of the flood are ultimately controlled by means of a dam in a gorge, the flow of thoughts, no matter how intimidating initially, can be brought to an end.

Appendix

What is *Advaita Vedānta?*

I

The discussion in this book is based on insights drawn from the school of Hindu philosophy known by the name of *Advaita Vedānta*. This appendix is intended for those who might wish to familiarize themselves a bit more with this system of Hindu philosophy.

Let us begin with the word itself, which perhaps appears formidably foreign when first encountered. It can however be de-exoticized quite easily with the help of a brief foray into philology. Let us take the word *Advaita* first. It can be broken up as *a-dvaita*. The initial *a* here has the same meaning as the letter *a* in ahistorical, that is, of negating what follows. Thus just as a-historical means not-historical, *a-dvaita* means not-*dvaita*.

But what does *dvaita* mean? This word is etymologically connected with the English word dual—a connection which can be phonetically heard if one says the two words *dvaita* and dual out aloud. The word *dvaita*, moreover, not only sounds like dual, but shares its meaning as well. Thus *dvaita* means dualism or "twoness." The word *Advaita* (*a-dvaita*) thus means not-two, or non-dual.

The word is however an adjective—so the question arises: what is it being applied to? In other words, about what is the claim being made that it is "not two"?

II

So let us put the word *Advaita* on hold for a moment and try to find out what the word which it qualifies means, namely *Vedānta*. The two can then be brought together again to reveal their meaning in its fullness.

The word *Vedānta* might also, like the word *Advaita*, appear forbiddingly alien at first sight. But once again it yields its meaning easily with the help of a mercifully brief excursion into philology.

The word *Vedānta* is made of two words—*veda* + *anta*. The word *veda* is derived from a root which means "to know"—the same root which appears in the three English words: wit, wisdom, and video, that is, to know intelligently (wit); to know sagely (wisdom); and to know visually (video). The word *veda*, derived from the same root *vid* (to know), denotes wisdom, that is to say, "spiritual" wisdom, and by implication the texts which embody that wisdom. Thus it is that the sacred scripture of the Hindus are called the *Vedas*, just as the sacred scripture of the Christians is known as the Bible, and of the Muslims as the Qur'ān. Note that unlike the Bible and the Qur'ān, the word *Veda* takes a plural ending. This is so because traditionally one speaks of the "four" *Vedas*, known as the *Ṛg-Veda*, the *Yajur-Veda*, the *Sāma-Veda,* and the *Atharva-Veda*. Sometimes, however, the word *Veda* is also used in the singular to refer to them collectively. The fact that, even to begin with, Hinduism possesses four sacred books and not just one tells us something about the inherently plural ethos of the tradition.

Not only are the *Vedas* four in number, four layers can be identified in each of them. The following chart may help clarify the picture in this respect.

Vedas

	Ṛg-	*Yajur-*	*Sāma-*	*Atharva-*
Mantra or *Saṁhitā*				
Brāhmaṇa				
Āraṇyaka				
Upaniṣad				

Each of the *Vedas* contains: (1) hymns (many shared by them in common) in praise of the gods; (2) prose explanations of the ritual use of these hymns; (3) reflections on the significance of ritual; and (4) secret texts meant to communicate the highest mysteries that go beyond ritual into the realm of spiritual knowledge. These layers are respectively called: (1) *Mantra* or *Saṁhitā* (i.e. hymns, or collections of hymns); (2) *Brāhmaṇa* (i.e. authoritative utterances of priests); (3) *Āraṇyaka* (i.e. forest-books); and (4) *Upaniṣad* (or mystic texts revealed to disciples as they sat up close to the masters). The rest of our presentation will focus on the *Upaniṣads*. Because they come at the end of the *Vedas*, or constitute the last of the four layers, they are also called *Vedānta*, that is, *Veda*'s end. The word *anta* in Sanskrit has the same meaning as the English word "end."

III

The texts which constitute the *Upaniṣads*, or *Vedānta*, deal with the central issues of philosophy: what is the ultimate reality about the universe around us, and about we who are asking this question? And what is the ultimate nature of this ultimate reality?

The *Upaniṣads*, more than two hundred of which have been identified, among which close to a dozen or more are considered the major ones, do not offer, at least on the face of it, a single answer to these questions. They are closer to being works of religious inspiration than systematic treatises on theology, and the inspired statements found therein lend themselves to many interpretations. Thus different schools of philosophy arose in India out of an attempt to present their teachings in a systematic way. These various schools of philosophy are known as schools of *Vedānta*, and they differ in their interpretation regarding the final teaching of the *Upaniṣads*. Thus questions such as: is the ultimate reality personal or impersonal in nature? are answered differently by these schools. Similarly, the schools differ in the answer they provide to such questions as: what is the relationship of the ultimate reality (*Brahman*) to the world? or what does realization consist of?

Advaita Vedānta is one such school of *Vedānta*. It is labeled *Advaita* because it does not ultimately regard either us or the universe as different from the ultimate reality—they are not two. It prefers to call them "not-two" rather than "one" because "not-two" implies a lack of fundamental division to begin with, whereas "one" may imply the coming together of two items that are in fact apart. Hence it prefers to speak in terms of an "undivided" (*a-dvaita*) Reality, in preference to one Reality, because according to it the positing of such a fundamental division is itself a product of error.

Are all living beings ultimately identical with *Brahman*? Is the universe also identical with it? Is there any difference between the way living beings are identical with *Brahman* and the way the universe is? If the ultimate reality is a single undivided reality, what reality do the different things and different people around us possess? Are they defilements or embellishments, and how can they exist without qualifying the undivided reality? The school of *Advaita Vedānta* tries its best to answer these questions by relying (1) on revelation, (2) on reason, and (3) on the teachings of those who are said to be living embodiments of the realization of *Brahman*.

Even as it attempts to answer our intellectual queries, *Advaita Vedānta* insists that the answer to our doubts cannot be fully found until the doubter is found out to be what he or she truly is. This is somewhat like saying that all the questions one might have about a dream, while one is in it, are finally cleared up only upon awakening from it. Hence the unrelenting focus of *Advaita Vedānta* on the personal realization of *Brahman* by the seeker. It is this emphasis that converts the philosophy of *Advaita Vedānta* into a spirituality.

A major issue this school of thought has to contend with is a not unexpected one: how to reconcile its claim of metaphysical non-dual reality with the apparent plurality of our empirical existence?

Here is a glimpse of the ways in which such a reconciliation might be proposed. The range of our experience in the empirical world is vertiginously diverse, but a little reflection suggests that all of it occurs in one of three states of consciousness: when one is awake, when one is dreaming, and while one is in deep sleep. These three states of experience provide a useful handle for talking of our empirical world because all the varied experiences we have in this world can be slotted within one of these three states of consciousness. Now in the waking state physical objects are real (at the empirical level). It can thus be described as *sat* or real. Compared to them objects and persons encountered in a dream are merely mental in nature and can thus be described as *cit*, or characterized by immaterial consciousness. Finally, the experience of deep sleep is universally considered restful, blissful, and happy. Thus this state of consciousness qualifies as *ānanda* or bliss. Thus the empirical reality we experience can be described as follows:

Waking	*Sat*
Dreaming	*Cit*
Deep Sleep	*Ānanda*

Readers will recall, however, that the ultimate reality, at the transcendental level, was also described in Part I of this book as *saccidānanda Brahman*, where *Brahman* denoted the ultimate reality to which the words *sat* (reality), *cit* (consciousness), and *ānanda* (bliss) are applied as ways of orienting ourselves towards it.

In other words, the question we are dealing with may be rephrased as follows: what is the relationship of the ultimate reality as *sat*, *cit*, and *ānanda* and our experience of the empirical world, which is also capable of being so described.

The question may be answered with the help of a chart.

Sat, Cit, Ānanda, Brahman

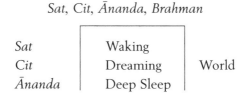

Sat	Waking	
Cit	Dreaming	World
Ānanda	Deep Sleep	

How could the horizontal line become the vertical, in other words? Just as a straight rod appears bent when placed in a tub full of water, says *Advaita Vedānta*. That is to say, there is something in the nature of the empirical world which apparently distorts the ultimate reality when viewed in relation with it. The word used to denote this "something" in *Advaita Vedānta* is *Māyā* or *Avidyā*.

But matters get straightened out when one achieves enlightenment. One way of moving towards such enlightenment or realization is to ask the question: if I undergo the experience of waking, dreaming, and deep sleep, which as states of consciousness differ so radically from one another, then how do I retain my sense of identity despite undergoing these different states of experience, and the different experiences I have within these states of waking, dreaming, and deep sleep. There must be some unchanging consciousness in me that undergirds my consciousness of change of these states of consciousness and the changes within them. Such unchanging consciousness is called *ātman* in *Advaita Vedānta*—which constitutes the unchanging core of our being.

According to *Advaita Vedānta* this *ātman* is identical with *Brahman*. They are not two. It is this understanding of non-dualism—that the *ātman* and *Brahman* are not two distinct entities but identically one—which represents experientially the most resonant dimension of *Advaitic* non-dualism. This is the truth, but somehow it has become warped and it is the goal of *Advaita Vedānta* to help us straighten it out.

Biographical Note

ARVIND SHARMA was born in Varanasi, India. He earned a B.A. in History, Economics, and Sanskrit from Allahabad University in 1958 and continued his interests in economics at Syracuse University, earning an M.A. in 1970. Pursuing a lifelong interest in comparative religion, Dr. Sharma gained an M.T.S. in 1974 and then a Ph.D. in Sanskrit and Indian Studies from Harvard University in 1978. He succeeded Wilfred Cantwell Smith to the Birks Chair of Comparative Religion at McGill University in Montreal, Canada and was the first Infinity Foundation Visiting Professor of Indic Studies at Harvard University. He has published over fifty books and five hundred articles in the fields of comparative religion, Hinduism, Indian philosophy and ethics, and the role of women in religion. Often cited as an authority on Hinduism, amongst his most noteworthy publications are *The Hindu Gita: Ancient and Classical Interpretations of the Bhagavadgita* (1986), *The Experiential Dimension of Advaita Vedanta* (1993), *Our Religions: The Seven World Religions Introduced by Preeminent Scholars from Each Tradition* (1994), and *The Study of Hinduism* (2003).

INDEX

For a glossary of all key foreign words used in books published by World Wisdom,
including metaphysical terms in English, consult:
www.DictionaryofSpiritualTerms.org.
This on-line Dictionary of Spiritual Terms provides extensive definitions, examples
and related terms in other languages.

Other Titles in the Perennial Philosophy Series by World Wisdom

Unveiling the Garden of Love:
Mystical Symbolism in Layla Majnun and Gita Govinda,
by Lalita Sinha, 2008

The Wisdom of Ananda Coomaraswamy:
Reflections on Indian Art, Life, and Religion,
edited by S. Durai Raja Singam and Joseph A. Fitzgerald, 2011

Wisdom's Journey: Living the Spirit of Islam in the Modern World,
by John Herlihy, 2009

Ye Shall Know the Truth: Christianity and the Perennial Philosophy,
edited by Mateus Soares de Azevedo, 2005

Books on Hinduism by World Wisdom

The Essential Sri Anandamayi Ma,
by Alexander Lipsky and Sri Anandamayi Ma, 2007

The Essential Swami Ramdas: Commemorative Edition,
compiled by Susunaga Weeraperuma, 2005

The Essential Vedanta: A New Source Book of Advaita Vedanta,
edited by Eliot Deutsch and Rohit Dalvi, 2004

A Guide to Hindu Spirituality,
by Arvind Sharma, 2006

Introduction to Hindu Dharma: Illustrated,
edited by Michael Oren Fitzgerald, 2007

Lamp of Non-Dual Knowledge & Cream of Liberation:
Two Jewels of Indian Wisdom,
translated by Swami Sri Ramanananda Saraswathi, 2003

The Original Gospel of Ramakrishna:
Based on M's English Text, Abridged,
edited by Swami Abhedananda and Joseph A. Fitzgerald, 2011

Paths to Transcendence:
According to Shankara, Ibn Arabi, and Meister Eckhart,
by Reza Shah-Kazemi, 2006

The Power of the Sacred Name:
Indian Spirituality Inspired by Mantras,
by V. Raghavan, 2011

Timeless in Time: Sri Ramana Maharshi,
by A.R. Natarajan, 2006

Tripura Rahasya: The Secret of the Supreme Goddess,
translated by Swami Sri Ramanananda Saraswathi, 2002

Unveiling the Garden of Love: Mystical Symbolism in
Layla Majnun & Gitagovinda,
by Lalita Sinha, 2007

The Wisdom of Ananda Coomaraswamy:
Reflections on Indian Art, Life, and Religion,
edited by S. Durai Raja Singam and Joseph A. Fitzgerald, 2011